Notes To My Daughter

A Story of Bonds So Strong, They Cannot Be Broken, Even In Death

JONI HEWITT

BALBOA PRESS
A DIVISION OF HAY HOUSE

Copyright © 2015 Joni Hewitt.

All rights reserved. No part of this book may be used or reproduced by any means, graphic, electronic, or mechanical, including photocopying, recording, taping or by any information storage retrieval system without the written permission of the author except in the case of brief quotations embodied in critical articles and reviews.

Front cover image by Anna Hewitt.

Balboa Press books may be ordered through booksellers or by contacting:

Balboa Press
A Division of Hay House
1663 Liberty Drive
Bloomington, IN 47403
www.balboapress.com
1 (877) 407-4847

Because of the dynamic nature of the Internet, any web addresses or links contained in this book may have changed since publication and may no longer be valid. The views expressed in this work are solely those of the author and do not necessarily reflect the views of the publisher, and the publisher hereby disclaims any responsibility for them.

The author of this book does not dispense medical advice or prescribe the use of any technique as a form of treatment for physical, emotional, or medical problems without the advice of a physician, either directly or indirectly. The intent of the author is only to offer information of a general nature to help you in your quest for emotional and spiritual well-being. In the event you use any of the information in this book for yourself, which is your constitutional right, the author and the publisher assume no responsibility for your actions.

Any people depicted in stock imagery provided by Thinkstock are models, and such images are being used for illustrative purposes only. Certain stock imagery © Thinkstock.

Print information available on the last page.

ISBN: 978-1-5043-4560-6 (sc)
ISBN: 978-1-5043-4562-0 (hc)
ISBN: 978-1-5043-4561-3 (e)

Library of Congress Control Number: 2015919624

Balboa Press rev. date: 12/15/2015

This book is dedicated to my daughter, Kelly. I love you, and I'm listening. Please don't stop showing up.

Contents

Introduction ix

Chapter 1	Someone Watching Over Me 1
Chapter 2	Angels And Spirit Guides 7
Chapter 3	Behind The Laughter 14
Chapter 4	Little Sister 20
Chapter 5	Angels Among Us 24
Chapter 6	The Next Battle 33
Chapter 7	August 43
Chapter 8	Dimes From Heaven 56
Chapter 9	Reasons To Believe 62
Chapter 10	The Dream 68
Chapter 11	I Am With You! 73
Chapter 12	Wanting More 78
Chapter 13	Let Me Go 89
Chapter 14	One More Reading 95
Chapter 15	Fly Away 100

Epilogue 105

Introduction

People say that the death of a child is the worst loss anyone can suffer. I used to hear it, but I never understood it. That is, until I lost my own child on August tenth, 2009. My daughter Kelly passed from this earth one week after her 34th birthday. How does a mother say goodbye to a child? It was the hardest thing I've ever had to do in my life. I couldn't do it. I found out that when your child dies, it doesn't matter how old that child may be—the pain is indescribable. And it never goes away.

I had lost people I loved before. My father and my dear grandmother who raised me from the age of eight had both passed seven years earlier. Although those were devastating losses, they didn't come close to the pain I felt upon the loss of my daughter.

When Kelly died, I couldn't let go of her. She had been a part of me since I was barely sixteen years old, still a child myself. With the help of my grandmother, Kelly and I had grown up together.

We were so close that I know something was taken from deep inside me when she passed. When I cried for my daughter, I would tell her that I just needed to know she was okay. I needed to know she was happy.

Then, a miracle happened. While I cried, Kelly heard me--and she responded. She began leaving me signs three days after her passing. Filled with hope, I poured my heart out in a journal of letters addressed to her. In them, I told her I didn't know how to go on without her. It was as if Kelly were reading the pages over my shoulder as I wrote. She responded over and over again through extraordinary signs that made me realize her spirit was with me.

But still, it wasn't enough. I went to one psychic medium after another.

Kelly was there for me every single time, telling me, "Yes, mom. I'm okay, and I'm happy."

During those readings, Kelly had messages of love for me and for the little sister who cried for her, too. My daughter, Anna, was six years old when Kelly died. She had been a diamond nugget shining brightly in Kelly's life, and Kelly didn't want Anna to forget how much she meant to her.

Before losing Kelly, I had been through several uncanny experiences in my life that made me question what was beyond the realms of our earthly existence. During those times, I had been comforted or received guidance from somewhere or someone that I couldn't explain. But Kelly proved to me—beyond any doubt—that life continues after the death of the body. My daughter reached from beyond the grave to pull me through my unbearable grief after losing her. And she didn't give up until she knew that I was going to be okay.

Kelly stayed with me for over three years after her death, answering my pleas and guiding me from the other side. It was Kelly who helped me move on after her death. She taught me that angels are real. She taught me that our love transcends the boundaries of this earth. And she showed me that the bond we shared cannot be broken—even in death. The same is true for the bonds shared by my daughters, my grandmother and me.

My daughter Kelly gave me the courage I needed to move forward in this life. I now know with certainty that we will be together again when the time is right. I am sharing the story of our journey with hopes that it may help someone else struggling through agonizing loss. I hope they too will find comfort in knowing that our losses are not final. They're not forever. We will see our loved ones again.

Chapter One

Someone Watching Over Me

"Hurry up, grandma! Hurry up, grandma!" The three of us held on to the top of the fence, swaying back and forth as we chanted.

A visit from Gram always made the day special. Standing on the low, white picket fence in our front yard, my bare feet between the pickets, I stretched my neck to keep the bus stop in view. My brother Jim who was just one year older than me, and my sister Judy who was seven, were with me. My younger sister, June, was still a baby so she stayed inside. I was four years old, and Gram was already a huge part of my life.

Then, the big, blue commuter bus pulled up to the stop, and Gram stepped down in her light pink nurse's aide uniform. I jumped up and down as I watched her walk down the street toward us with a big, loving smile on her face. I remember her chestnut brown hair pulled back loosely to frame her beautiful face. She was still stunning at fifty years old.

The four of us children were raised as Catholics. We attended Catholic school and each made our First Holy Communion at St. Leo's Church. I remember it being a big deal. A picture of devotion, I practiced saying my prayers every night to prepare for the big day. When it finally arrived, I felt like a miniature bride in my white dress and long veil.

It was very shortly after my communion that my parents split up. They had horrible battles with lots of screaming and yelling. During those arguments, I would run up the stairs to my room, and hide deep under the covers of my bed. I held my hands over my ears while I hummed a song, waiting for the screaming to stop.

Once, I remember falling asleep while hiding there, and being awakened by someone calling my name.

I heard it very clearly. "Joni! Joni! It's okay."

I sat up in the bed and looked around to see who was calling my name. But I was alone in the room. I was positive I had not imagined what I heard. I sat there for a moment wondering where the voice had come from. Who had said my name? A shiver went up my spine as I pulled the covers up over my head once more, and peered from beneath them. I never shared that eerie experience with anyone, but I never forgot it. I know someone had been in that room with me.

It wasn't long after that experience that my sisters, brother, and I moved out of our comfortable, two-story home and into a run-down duplex with my mother. She was a far cry from the perfect mother. The only attention we received was when she yelled at us for not cleaning the house well enough. Since she worked nights as a bartender, we had to get ourselves up and off to school each morning while she slept. I was in third grade at the time. I made myself breakfast, and wore the same dirty clothes to school each day.

Then one day we came home from school, and our mother was gone.

My sister, Judy, was responsible for making the call to the bar each day after school to tell my mother we were home. This particular day in May, the person on the other end of the line told Judy my mother had not shown up for work that day. Judy hung up the phone and immediately called Gram to see if she might know where our mother was. Gram told Judy that she would try and find out, and call us back. The four of us huddled in a circle around the phone waiting for Gram to call. When the phone rang, Judy answered.

I don't know what Gram's exact words to my sister were, but Judy turned to look at me with tears welling up in her eyes. Then she screamed, "Mommy left us!"

I remember immediately bursting into tears, and we all stood there crying as Judy hung up the phone. Gram and dad arrived a short time later, and took us to Gram's house. I was eight years old, and from that day on, Gram became my mother.

We moved to a rough neighborhood on the lower west side of Cleveland. The stench of the nearby steel mill where most people earned a living always hung in the air. Religion was an important part of our life with Gram. One of my favorite childhood memories is of lying in bed at night with Gram saying our prayers. I can still hear her voice reciting the *Our Father,* or teaching me how to pray the rosary.

Gram worked full time as a nurses' aide, and would then come home and care for us. My father was with us some of the time, but Gram was the one who raised us. It was a hard life for her, but she never made us feel like a burden.

After my mother left, I always felt unworthy of love. I couldn't help but notice the other kids at school had their mothers involved in every aspect of their lives. I wondered why my own mother hadn't loved me enough to stay. As a teenager, I was unsupervised a lot after school, and I got mixed up with the wrong crowd. I began cutting classes and staying out too late. It was then that I met a tough guy from the neighborhood who was a couple years older than me. He paid attention to me, and I thought I was in love. I had my first sexual encounter at the young age of fifteen. I remember being terrified, and I stopped him after just a few seconds. But those few seconds were all it took.

The following month, I missed my period. I kept waiting and praying it would start, but it never did. Gram knew that I was late, and she was angry. We took the long bus ride to the doctor's office together in silence. I was a scared little girl in a Rolling Stones t-shirt, and torn up jeans, when the doctor confirmed the worst—I was pregnant. My head began to spin, and I felt like I would be sick right there under the bright, fluorescent lights that glared down on me. Instead, I sat on the examining table and cried.

I remember thinking, "How can this be possible? I had stopped him within seconds. How can I be pregnant?"

Gram's anger quickly turned to tenderness, and she hugged me lovingly, telling me not to worry.

Gram said, "We'll take care of it together."

A few months into my pregnancy, a social worker visited me. She convinced me the best thing to do for the baby—and myself—would be adoption. The boy I had been so crazy about had disappeared the minute I told him I was pregnant. I was no longer in school, and I had no idea how I was going to care for the new life I felt growing inside of me. I thought the social worker was right. Gram did not agree. She was furious with me when I told her of my plan. The last thing she wanted was for me to give up my baby. Gram was willing to do whatever it took to help me, and she told me so.

Gram said, "We can do this together."

I wasn't feeling the same confidence Gram was feeling. The months went by, and I was soon due for my nine-month check-up. I saw a doctor at the clinic inside the hospital where Gram still worked as a nurse's aide. The day of my appointment, I took the bus by myself and arrived at the clinic early. As I took my seat in the waiting room, I noticed a new mother sitting across from me. She smiled when our eyes met. Her newborn was next to her in a rolling hospital bassinet. I stood up and timidly walked over to the bassinet to get a closer look at her baby. I peered down at the miniature form tightly swaddled in a soft, pink blanket, and I saw a tiny face staring back at me. At that moment, an overwhelming feeling of certainty came over me. I swear, the precious little girl in the bassinet smiled up at me as if she knew all along what I, myself, had just realized. I made the decision at that moment. I was going to keep my baby. The next morning, I went into labor.

After 27 hours of agonizing labor, my daughter Kelly was born. I'll never forget the first moment I laid eyes on her. I took in every detail from her perfectly round head to her long, slender legs. She had olive skin, dark hair, and big, dark brown eyes. There was a tiny mole on her neck that reminded me of a chocolate chip that had melted there. Kelly was perfect. As I stared, mesmerized by her beauty, I felt a love more powerful than anything I had ever experienced. My whole life changed in an instant, and I realized nothing else would ever be as important as this. I had become a teen mom.

When it was time for Kelly and me to go home, Gram helped take care of Kelly, just as she had promised. When Kelly was around three months old, her cries awakened me in the middle of the night. When I picked her up, I realized she was running a very high fever. Her face was fiery red, and her tender skin felt blazing to the touch. I was in a panic, and I quickly ran to wake Gram. I stood by biting my nails while Gram expertly filled the kitchen sink, and then gently lowered Kelly's tiny, unclothed body into the tepid water. Gram soothingly splashed the water onto Kelly's body using a small washcloth, slowly wiping her brow and limbs. I don't know what I would have done if Gram had not been there to teach me how to be a mother.

Chapter Two

Angels And Spirit Guides

The year progressed, and I adjusted to my new role as mom. I was no longer the rebellious teenager that stayed out too late with friends. I was home at night, caring for my daughter. Kelly was an exceptionally good baby, crying only when she was hungry or sick. Even at a few months old, I noticed how much she enjoyed her bath time. Kelly would wiggle with contentment as I massaged baby lotion all over her back or brushed what little hair she had with the soft bristled baby brush. Kelly loved to be touched and held.

When Kelly was one year old, I became involved with another guy from my neighborhood that I had known for years. We were married in front of a judge in a quick ceremony. Within a few short months, I realized I had made a huge mistake.

On more than one occasion during that brief marriage, I remember laying in bed at night and experiencing the feeling of actually leaving my body. I would be soaring over oceans, mountains, and marching armies. I felt like a bird flying over the earth taking in the sites below. I later learned that this is a phenomenon referred to as astral travel. I think it was my subconscious way of escaping a terrible situation. I filed for divorce, and the marriage was over before my son Jimmy was born. I was eighteen years old, living on my own with one small child, and pregnant.

Kelly had just celebrated her second birthday when a social worker paid us a visit. Kelly sat in the middle of the living room on the brand new orange tricycle Gram had bought for her. I sat down on the couch next to the social worker.

As Kelly sat on her bike, she began to sing, "Happy birthday to me."

I had fixed Kelly's hair into two high ponytails, and she looked adorable singing her song while trying to peddle the bike. The social worker and I both paused to smile and watch the priceless show Kelly performed for us. Afterward, the social worker quickly explained the reason for her visit. She said she wanted to help us get on our feet. She appeared to be a kind woman, and I was very grateful to hear those words. I told her that I had always wanted to be a secretary. She offered to look into clerical training programs available to me.

I gave birth to my son two months later. Kelly, Jimmy and I were living in a run down apartment complex several blocks away from Gram. Oftentimes, I would place Jimmy into his simple umbrella stroller, gather Kelly into my arms, and walk to Gram's house for a meal. I carried Kelly in one arm while pushing the stroller with my free hand. When Kelly became too heavy, I would put her down to walk. I pushed the stroller slowly so her tiny legs could keep up with me. Kelly was so little, but she never cried as she toddled quietly behind me. We survived on public assistance and the care packages Gram sent home with us after our visits.

As I became older and wiser, or maybe just tougher, I resolved to get out of that life. I knew in my heart that my children and I deserved something better. Although I always kept our home clean and took good care of my kids, I knew we needed more. And the only way I could achieve that was by finding a job.

The social worker had sent information to me on a clerical training program offered in my neighborhood. I looked through the paperwork and called the number listed. Within a few months of Jimmy's birth, I was attending clerical training classes. Each morning, I took the bus to a nearby daycare center to drop Kelly and Jimmy off. Then I would catch the next bus that took me to the training center. At the same time, I took night classes to earn my high school diploma while Gram watched the kids. I completed a six-month clerical training program, and was twenty years old when I began my first job with an insurance company located in downtown Cleveland. I stayed with that company for the next sixteen years. I worked hard and was promoted quickly.

Within a couple of years, Kelly, Jimmy and I moved into a cozy, downstairs unit of a duplex in our neighborhood. Eventually, I was able to get a car, which made it much easier to get around. When Gram retired from her job at the hospital, she moved into the unit above us. It was a perfect situation. Kelly began kindergarten at the Catholic school located on the corner of our street. Gram walked to pick Kelly up each day after school, and spend the afternoon hours with her until I returned from work. Jimmy was enrolled in a daycare program at the local community center, and I would drop him off on my way downtown. During this time, Kelly was forming the same special bond with Gram that Gram and I had shared my entire life.

I was learning to be a mother as I was growing up. Working a full-time job and being a single mother to two small children was not easy. I'm so lucky and grateful that I had Gram to help us. Still, there were times when I would lose my patience with Kelly and Jimmy, and yell at them. I hated myself for that because it reminded me of my own mother; the mother I never wanted to be. I made a vow to myself that no matter how hard my life became I would never desert my children. Being abandoned by my own mother had left a permanent scar on my heart. How does a mother do that? That was something I would never understand. So, I tried to be the best mother I could be to my precious babies. Kelly was a bright, outgoing little girl who made friends very easily. She was also a very affectionate child, and would say, "I love you, Mommy," several times each day.

I would respond, "I love you, too, Kelly."

I would tuck Kelly and Jimmy into their beds each night, read them a bedtime story, and afterwards, they would say their prayers.

Before I turned out the lights each night in the room they shared, I would say, "Goodnight! Sleep tight! Don't let the bed bugs bite!" as they smiled at me from underneath their covers.

I still said my own prayers before I went to bed each night as Gram had taught me.

NOTES TO MY DAUGHTER

I would always end my prayers with the same request, "Dear God, please help me be a good mother to my children. Keep them safe from harm always."

By the time Kelly was ten years old, and Jimmy was eight, we had moved into a single, two-story home. They each had their own room and although Gram wasn't living above us any longer, we saw her often. I managed to keep Kelly and Jimmy in Catholic school every year on my modest salary, and they were both doing well at their studies. Kelly was twelve when she joined the school basketball team. I was thrilled that she showed an interest in sports, but I missed a lot of her games because they were usually held right after school while I was still at work.

One night, I tucked Jimmy into bed then walked across the hall to Kelly's room to find her crying.

When I asked Kelly what was wrong, she replied, "Mom, I wish you could be at more of my games. The other mothers are always there. I scored a point for our team today, and you weren't even there to see it."

I felt terribly guilty, and I said, "I'm sorry, Kelly. I do want to be there, but sometimes it's impossible when I have to be at work all day."

Kelly responded with a slight smile, and mumbled, "I understand, Mom."

I kissed her goodnight and watched as she turned away from me to face the wall. I understood what she was feeling. She wanted her mom there all the time. I wished I didn't have to work full time so I could be there more. I hated that my kids let themselves into an empty house each day after school. The few times that I was able to take days off to attend field trips with them weren't enough, but they had to do.

Overall, Kelly was a happy kid, always surrounded by a lot of friends. The three of us were doing pretty well, and Gram was never far away when we needed her. Then, I became involved in another bad relationship. I really had a knack for picking the worst.

Kelly didn't like this guy, and she told me so. When we were alone, she would say, "Why are you with him? I hate him and I don't want him here!"

Kelly was right. I didn't want him there either and I was trying to get out of the relationship. One day, I was taking my lunch break in the park next to our office building. I was sitting alone on the park bench when a man sat down next to me and started a conversation. He was around my age, and nice looking. As we talked, he asked if I was seeing anyone. I told him I was in a relationship that I was trying to end.

He responded by saying, "You are a beautiful woman. You could have anything you want in life. Don't let this guy stop you because you deserve so much more."

With that, he stood up, warmly shook my hand and walked away. A peculiar feeling came over me afterward. I felt as if this man knew everything about me, and that he somehow shared my deepest secrets. His words gave me the strength I needed. Shortly after that day, I was able to get up the courage to end the relationship. I often thought about that guy in the park. I felt as though he had been an angel sent down from Heaven to guide me, and I was grateful. I wished I had watched him more closely as he walked away. Maybe I would have seen his wings.

Shorty after ending the relationship, I had another uncanny experience. The owner of the house the kids and I were renting sold the place and we had to find somewhere else to live. After a long search, I found a new home for us, but the rent was much higher. I was struggling to make ends meet, and it was a difficult time for us. I sat in the darkness of my room late one night crying, asking God when something good was going to happen in our lives. At that moment, I heard a loud, clear response in my head that said, "Go to California."

There was no mistaking what I heard. Someone had responded to my pleas, and I listened. A few days later, I went to California to visit my sister, Judy, who had moved there several years earlier. While visiting Judy, I met a man named Ron who would become my husband. Within six months, Kelly, Jimmy and I moved to California to start a new life.

Chapter Three

Behind The Laughter

Ron turned out to be the finest husband and father to my children I could ever have imagined. Ron's three sons, Ronnie, Jeff and Kevin were close in age to Kelly and Jimmy, and we were working through the challenge of blending our two families. The company I worked for transferred me to our Los Angeles office, which meant I had a long commute into downtown each day. I spent hours away from home while Kelly and Jimmy tried to adjust to their new surroundings. The transition wasn't easy for either of them, but it was harder on Kelly. She was thirteen years old, which was already a tough age for girls. Kelly had left a lot of good friends and a school she loved. Her new school was a vastly different environment than what she was used to in our small suburb of Cleveland.

Kelly cried, and told me, "I want to go back home."

I knew it was hard on Kelly, and I tried my best to help her adjust. Within a few months, she was doing well, and had several new friends. People were drawn to her outgoing nature and wacky sense of humor. I was relieved to see Kelly smiling again.

Although Kelly and I had the typical teenage mother/daughter battles over curfews or boys, the love we shared never waivered.

After an argument, Kelly would come to me and say, "I'm sorry, Mom."

Then, she would lay her head in my lap as we sat on the couch and I would brush her hair. That small act of tenderness still calmed her just as it had when she was a baby.

I remember one day when Kelly was about 15 years old. She was hanging out in her room with a friend when I passed by her door. Kelly called out to me so I turned and went back to stand in the doorway.

Kelly smiled and said, "Wait, I want to play a song for you!"

"Okay," I said as I smiled in return.

Kelly played Bette Midler's *Wind Beneath My Wings* while I stood there listening.

When the song finished playing, Kelly smiled lovingly at me and said, "That's my song to you, Mommy."

I was deeply touched, and my face began to feel flushed as Kelly watched my reaction. The lyrics to the song were a beautiful testimonial of Kelly's love for me.

I walked over to where Kelly sat on the bed and hugged her tightly. "Thank you," I said.

I left the room with a smile on my face. I thought maybe I was doing something right! It was a heartwarming feeling to know that my teenage daughter loved me that much.

It was after graduating high school that Kelly joined in the California obsession with tanning salons. I didn't like them, and when she came home with a tanning membership, I let her know that I didn't approve.

"Kelly they aren't good for you!" I would argue.

Kelly had the typical carefree attitude that most of us have when we're young that we are invincible.

Her response was always the same, "Oh, mom. Don't worry. They are perfectly safe."

It never felt right to me, and I continued to voice my concerns on deaf ears. Kelly continued to tan from her late teens all through her twenties.

I wish I had been more persistent in my objections.

Kelly was too busy enjoying life to worry. She loved to laugh, and her boisterous chortle was contagious. Kelly would have people laughing uncontrollably, myself included, when she did impressions of different guests on the Jerry Springer Show. Her antics were hilarious.

Although she was laughing on the outside, Kelly began to show signs of deep depression. She was so sensitive that whenever she heard certain songs on the radio like R.E.M's *Everybody Hurts*, or Christina Aquilera's *Beautiful*, she would cry.

I would see the tears and ask, "Why are you so sad?"

Kelly could never bring herself to answer, but I saw the sadness that always seemed to be there just under the surface. I took her to doctors who prescribed medication for depression.

Each time, she would stop taking the medication after awhile, saying she didn't need it.

Kelly was diagnosed with Bipolar Disorder and severe depression when she was in her mid-twenties. She continued the same pattern of starting and stopping her medication. It became a vicious cycle of happiness and depression. At first, I didn't understand Bipolar Disorder.

I was so naïve that I used to tell Kelly, "Just try and be happy and you will be."

Eventually, I learned that a person being tormented by this horrific disease is incapable of just making it go away. It is pure torture for the person constantly battling for happiness each day. It is also devastating for the people that love them and are powerless to help.

Kelly refused to let her disease keep her down for long. She really did want to be happy. If we were in the car together when one of our favorite songs came on the radio, we would crank up the volume, and the two of us would belt out the song at the top of our lungs. We were having fun and we didn't care who heard us.

When Kelly started a new job in L.A., she was ready to move out on her own. She was working in the music industry, and moving up quickly. I was proud of her strong work ethic. We found a great apartment in a trendy area of Hollywood, and we decorated her place together with pieces we found in the local antique stores. Kelly had the coolest sense of style; not only in the things she chose to decorate her apartment, but also in the way she dressed. I was amazed at how Kelly could walk into one of the second hand stores down on Melrose Avenue and walk out with the coolest outfit she had thrown together in a flash.

Some days, Kelly would call me and say, "Come out for lunch tomorrow, Mom. I found a great new restaurant I want you to try!"

We also loved a lot of the same music. Many times, Kelly would get tickets to see a band we both loved and we would go to the show together. Sometimes, one of Kelly's many friends would join us.

I remember telling Kelly, "You have so many friends I can't keep track of their names!"

Although Kelly's life was full of friends that loved her, she and I were best friends. If we weren't together, we talked on the phone several times each day. When there was something new and exciting happening in Kelly's life, I was the first one she called. It was an exciting time for her on the outside, but inside, Kelly continued the battle to find happiness.

I was taken by surprise the day Kelly came to me and said, "I've joined Alcoholics Anonymous."

I asked, "Is your drinking that serious, Kelly."

"Yes, Mom. It is. And it's more than just drinking. I need help and I think this will be good for me."

I told Kelly that I was proud of her honesty and bravery, and that we would get through it together. I had no idea how bad it had been for her. Kelly had been very good at shielding me from the severity of the internal battle she was fighting. She had been self-medicating for a long time, and I wondered how I could have been so blind. The AA program did turn out to be really good for Kelly. She made many new friends at the nightly meetings she attended regularly. After awhile, Kelly was even brave enough to share her own story in front of the group.

Kelly slipped more than once and dropped out of the AA program. But, she always went back as she courageously fought to find happiness. It was a very difficult time for Kelly, and more than once, she attempted to take her own life. As a parent, it was devastating to watch my child suffer and be unable to help her. Ron and I tried. We admitted Kelly into treatment centers several times as she tried to be rid of the heartless disease. But, it refused to set her free.

Kelly would tell me, "Mom, I'm not going to live to be old." My response was always, "Stop it, Kelly! Yes, you will."

Chapter Four

Little Sister

Kelly began feeling powerless over her illness the same year Gram passed away. Gram was 88 years old and suffered from Alzheimer's disease when we lost her. Kelly was the first person I called after receiving the news of Gram's passing from her caregiver.

When Kelly answered her phone, I blurted out, "Gram died!"

Kelly began to cry and quickly muttered, "I'm on my way."

When Kelly arrived at the house, we sat at the kitchen table together, held hands and cried. We both loved Gram so much that neither of us could imagine our lives without her being part of it.

Kelly said, "Mom, what are we going to do without Gram?"

I shook my head. I didn't have an answer. I thought losing Gram was the worst thing I would ever have to experience.

It was about one year after Gram's passing when I read an article in the newspaper about a little boy who had died at the hands of his foster parents. It was heartbreaking, like so many stories in the news are. But for some reason, I couldn't get this particular story out of my head. Shortly after I read the article, I began to get a nagging feeling that I needed to do foster care. I didn't understand why or where it was coming from. Ron and I had finished raising our kids. They were all grown up, living their lives. Getting Kelly well was my main focus. I pushed the nagging feeling aside.

But it wasn't long before the nagging returned, this time with a stronger sense of urgency. I couldn't get it out of my head—*You need to do foster care, you need to do foster care!* Something, or someone, definitely wanted me to do it. Finally, I relented.

I walked into Ron's office, and announced, "I think I need to do foster care."

Ron, in his usual supportive manner, replied, " If that's what you need to do, you should do it."

"Okay, I'm doing it!" I responded.

It was so serendipitous the way everything happened from that point on. It was as if someone else had taken the wheel and I was no longer in control. Things just played out the way they were meant to be.

Within a month after completing the necessary training and background checks to become a qualified foster parent, I received a call from the county. They had a five-month old baby girl named Anna they wanted to bring to me. She was to stay with us while an adoptive family was located. I remember the day the county brought Anna to us. Kelly was the only one at the house with me when the social worker arrived. I greeted her at the door and she came in with the baby carrier in her hand. We watched her place the carrier down in front of the couch, and Kelly and I smiled as we moved closer to see the baby girl inside. Anna was beautiful. She had dark eyes, radiant olive skin, and jet-black hair. She reminded me of Kelly when she was a baby. Kelly was 28 years old at the time, and she adored Anna from the moment she laid eyes on her. She couldn't wait to have kids of her own once she found the right guy. That hadn't happened yet because Kelly had a knack for picking the bad boys; a trait, I fear, she inherited from me.

I quickly got into a routine of taking care of a baby again. One night, after Anna had been with us for several months, she awakened me to be fed. We sat together in the rocking chair in the corner of her darkened room while she drank from the bottle I had warmed. It was the wee hours of the morning, and the only light came from the moon shining through the blind on the window. Once Anna finished eating, I placed her against my shoulder, and patted her back while rocking her back to sleep. Then, something incredible happened. I felt a jolt go between our two hearts as Anna lay on my chest. It's hard to describe the sensation other than it literally felt like a zap from her heart directly to mine. I had never experienced anything like that with Kelly and Jimmy, the children I had given birth to myself. With Anna, I truly believe it was at that exact moment we bonded, and our hearts became permanently connected. It was a miraculous moment for me—I felt the sheer power of love.

I received a phone call later that month from a woman with the state. She said that she wanted to schedule an appointment to do the in-home assessment required before we could officially adopt Anna. The comment took me by surprise, and I explained that we were temporary foster parents. She quickly apologized, and we hung up. I remember thinking how odd that call had been. Why had she assumed we were to be adoptive parents? Again, it was as if the events transpiring were completely out of my control. Someone knew what I was supposed to be doing even if I hadn't figured it out yet.

Finally, I realized that Anna was already where she belonged—with us. It made complete sense given the amount of love we had for Anna in our hearts! Ron and I began the adoption process and Anna became part of our family forever. I didn't understand why, but I felt very strongly that Gram had something to do with this plan.

Anna became the one light in Kelly's life. Kelly came to the house whenever she could get away from her job in L.A. to play with Anna, or just snuggle with her on the couch watching one of Anna's animated films. *Shrek* was a favorite. Kelly bought Anna a funny looking *Shrek* doll that she carried around for months, never letting it out of her sight.

They had a favorite game they played every time Kelly walked in the front door.

Anna would yell out, "Chase me!"

Then, Kelly would drop her green duffel bag full of laundry at the front door, and chase Anna throughout the house as Anna squealed with delight. I loved watching the two of them bring so much happiness to each other. Everyone who knew Kelly could see the joy that Anna brought to her life. Kelly would tell me that Anna was the only reason she got out of bed in the morning.

Chapter Five

Angels Among Us

A big part of the Alcoholics Anonymous credo is that members choose their own higher power to pray to for strength. Kelly chose Gram as hers. Kelly even had a beautiful portrait of Gram encircled by a rosary tattooed on her left arm as a special tribute to her. Kelly was very much like Gram. It seemed she was always taking in some tortured soul that she would meet at an AA meeting to crash on her couch. I told Kelly that she needed to focus on getting herself better before she could help others. She never listened. Just like Gram, she always thought there was someone out there who needed help more than she did.

Kelly would say, "She has nowhere to go. It's only for a little while."

I would respond, "Sure, Kelly."

It felt right to me that Kelly had chosen Gram as her higher power. I knew the bond they shared, and I felt strongly that Gram's spirit had not died when she left this earth. I knew this because Gram had visited me in a dream eight months after her passing. She stood in front of me very clearly with her arms folded in front of her. Her gray hair was pulled up and away from her face, the way she had worn it the last few months of her life. On Gram's face was a smile that is hard to describe. The smile was neither happy nor sad. She didn't say a word, but looked directly at me. I knew she was trying to tell me something.

At the time of the dream, my father was living with Ron and me under hospice care. He had been doing better, and Jimmy offered to stay at the house that night to look after him. Ron and I were away celebrating our wedding anniversary. My father passed away one hour after Ron and I returned home that day. As I cried for my father, I realized that Gram had been trying to tell me her son needed me at home.

During the time Kelly was praying to Gram for strength, she began finding dimes. She would sit down at an AA meeting and find a dime on the table in front her. She would get out of her car and find a dime sitting on her seat. The dimes appeared often enough to know that it couldn't be a coincidence. When Kelly told me about the dimes, it immediately brought to mind a book I had read years earlier entitled *Hello From Heaven*. The book told stories of people that had received messages from their loved ones who had passed. I remembered reading about how, often times, they would leave pennies or dimes. That one brief paragraph in the book had always stuck in my mind.

I shared this memory with Kelly. I told her Gram must be acknowledging her prayers, and letting her know she was listening! Kelly wanted to believe it was true, but she had her doubts. In her mind, Gram didn't seem to be giving her the strength she had been asking for. Then, something miraculous happened that would leave no doubt in Kelly's mind that Gram was with her.

Kelly was at a late night AA meeting in Hollywood that she attended regularly. This particular night, Kelly decided to get up and share in front of the group. While Kelly spoke, she noticed an elderly woman sitting in the audience. Kelly had never seen this woman before at this meeting or any of the other meetings she attended around town. She noticed that the whole time she spoke, the woman's gaze never left her. The woman listened very intently, and would smile whenever Kelly looked her way. Once Kelly finished speaking, she walked directly into the ladies' room to regroup. It can be very difficult to get up and share your story and your struggles in front of an audience, and Kelly had been very brave. Kelly was standing at the sink when the elderly woman walked into the room. She walked right up to Kelly and expressed how proud she was of her for being able to share.

As they spoke, the woman introduced herself to Kelly and said," My name is Gizzella."

Kelly stared at the woman in disbelief as she softly said, "That was my grandmother's name."

Gizzella was the name given to Gram by her parents who had emigrated to the U.S. from Hungary in 1912. As an adult, Gram changed her name to Elizabeth, and began going by its shortened version, Betty. Both Kelly and I remembered Gram's story of how she had changed her given name to the name she had chosen for her Catholic Confirmation. Gram always ended her story by giving us the correct pronunciation and spelling of Gizzella.

The woman replied, "I know, dear," as she smiled and gently touched Kelly's arm.

Kelly stared at the tiny woman in wonderment while she continued with, "Don't worry. You're going to be just fine."

With that, the kindhearted woman said goodbye, turned and left the room. Kelly stood there for a moment trying to grasp the wondrous moment she had just experienced. Then, she immediately went to her car and called me to relay the events.

Kelly's voice was shaking as she told me the story. I listened in amazement.

The first thing I remember saying to Kelly when she finished was, "Oh My God, Kelly!"

Then I said, "Kelly, it was Gram! I don't think she can make it any clearer to you that she's listening. She hears your prayers, and she's sending you the strength that you're asking her for."

Even though I was saying those words to Kelly, I couldn't believe what she had just told me! I was in awe of the wonderment of the experience. As I hung up the phone, I asked myself, *how could this even be possible? Had Gram really just visited Kelly, her spirit in human form?*

From then on, there was little doubt in Kelly's mind that Gram was with her. Neither Kelly nor I had any idea what was to come next, and that Kelly would soon need Gram's strength more than we had ever imagined.

Kelly at age four, and Jimmy at age two, with me in the background

Kelly on her sixth birthday with her cousin Angie

My beautiful Gram at age 83

Kelly and me together at a friend's party in 2002

Jimmy and me

Our family on vacation in Maui in 2008. Front row: Our grandkids Avery, Sadie, Hayden and Mason. 2nd Row: Our daughter-in-law Megan, son Jeff, granddaughters Kaytlin and Camryn, me, holding Anna (who was hiding from the camera), our daughter-in-law Teresa and son Kevin. Back Row: Daughter-in-law Kelly, son Ronnie, My Kelly (right beside me), Jimmy and Ron

Anna dressed up as Cinderella for Halloween with her special Shrek doll from Kelly. He went everywhere with her

Kelly and me baking Christmas cookies in 2001 - something we did together every year

Ron and Anna on a trip to Cabo

Kelly with Anna on our trip to Playa Del Carmen in 2007

Chapter Six

The Next Battle

Anna was five-years old when I noticed Kelly beginning to sleep more than usual. At that time, Kelly was taking some time off from work. Bipolar Disease had finally gotten the best of her. I won't say that Kelly ever gave up the fight because that would be untrue. She was trying to get healthy, and her hectic work schedule became too much. She was back to seeing her doctor regularly and taking her medication. She would sleep in late each day and I would eventually call to wake her.

Some days, Kelly would drive to our house to hang out with Anna and do her laundry. She returned to Hollywood in the evenings to attend a meeting. When Kelly walked though the front door, she and Anna still played their silly chase game. Anna laughed and took off running through the house with Kelly close on her heels. But, I noticed Kelly would be fast asleep on the couch shortly after her arrival. The mother in me was concerned as I watched Kelly sleep, but I knew she was on a lot of medication. I thought it was the effects of that, along with her depression making her sleep so much. I also thought the fatigue could be a lack of iron, so I suggested to Kelly that she have her doctor check her iron levels. During this time, Kelly also began complaining about pain in her lower back.

In January 2009, Kelly, Anna, Jimmy and I went to lunch at one of Kelly's favorite eateries in Hollywood. After we ordered, I couldn't help but notice the paleness of Kelly's skin and the big dark circles underneath her eyes. Kelly didn't look well. It appeared to be an effort just picking up her fork.

I was worried and I asked, "Kelly, how are you feeling?"

Kelly responded, "All I want to do is sleep. I'm tired all the time."

Again, I brought up her iron levels and asked, "Has the doctor run any blood tests?"

Kelly said her routine blood work had checked out fine. I suggested that Kelly have them check her iron levels one more time.

The pain in Kelly's back became increasingly worse so she began seeing a chiropractor. I suffered with lower back pain my whole life and visited my chiropractor regularly for adjustments. I didn't find her back pain to be anything out of the ordinary and thought the adjustments would help her. A year earlier, Kelly had been involved in a car accident and had visited my chiropractor several times afterward. I thought the recurring pain could be attributed to that accident.

Kelly was now seeing a chiropractor near her apartment in Hollywood. He took an x-ray of her back and concluded that Kelly had a bulging disc in her lower back that was causing the pain. She continued with adjustments for the next five months, but instead of finding relief, the pain was becoming unbearable. I was getting more and more concerned.

It was a Thursday in early May when Kelly came to the house after her chiropractor appointment. She pulled up the back of her shirt to show me the "bulging disc" on her lower back. I was horrified by what I saw. There was a growth the size of a golf ball protruding from Kelly's back at the base of her spine.

My hand went to my mouth and I said, "Oh my God, Kelly! What are they saying about that?"

Kelly again told me that the growth was being referred to as a bulging disc. But, the chiropractor was now saying another possibility could be something called a hematoma. I learned that a hematoma is a buildup of blood in an area that had been injured which causes swelling. Kelly did not recall injuring her back, and told the chiropractor so. Since it had now been five months of adjustments with no relief, Kelly's chiropractor scheduled an MRI for the next day. I was relieved Kelly would finally be getting a more thorough check.

When Kelly left the house that day, I hugged her and she said, "I'll see you Sunday, Mom."

Sunday was Mothers' Day, and Ron was going to barbeque steaks on the grill. As I watched Kelly drive away that day, I couldn't help but feel uneasy. Something just wasn't right. Why was nothing relieving her pain? And I couldn't get the image of that "bulging disc" out of my head.

When Sunday arrived, Kelly called to wish me a happy Mothers' Day and I thanked her. Then she apologized, saying her back was bothering her so badly that she wasn't going to be able to make the drive out. She just wanted to stay home in bed. I completely understood and told her not to worry. I wanted her to rest. I knew that she was expecting the results of the MRI the next day, and told her to call me the minute she heard anything.

The phone rang at 5:00 P.M. that Monday afternoon. I saw Kelly's name appear on my caller I.D. and answered immediately.

I still remember Kelly's words very clearly, and the shakiness in her voice when she said, "They're talking cancer."

A soundless dread came over me as I slowly pulled out a chair at the kitchen table and sat down.

"What do you mean, Kelly?"

Kelly told me that the results showed what appeared to be cancer in her lower back. Her chiropractor said it wasn't positive, and he was sending her to a surgeon who would perform a biopsy. Neither Kelly nor I had ever even considered the possibility of cancer. Her chiropractor had said it was a bulging disc. We had both assumed he knew what he was talking about.

Kelly said, "It can't be cancer."

"You're right," I said. "It can't be cancer. It would have come up in the blood work you've been having regularly to monitor your medication."

Or so I thought. I tried to put Kelly at ease by saying it was probably a hematoma as the chiropractor had suggested earlier. I told Kelly that I would pick her up for the appointment with the surgeon the next day and not to worry. But as I hung up the phone, I couldn't shake the feeling of trepidation that crept over me.

Ron came in from work just as Kelly and I were finishing our conversation. I looked at him and said, "That was Kelly. They're talking cancer."

Ron stared back at me blankly, neither of us knowing what to say next. I had never suspected cancer. This couldn't possibly be happening after everything Kelly was already going through. I was overcome by a feeling of nausea relaying everything Kelly had said to Ron. Was this someone's idea of a sick joke? Kelly wasn't strong enough to deal with cancer, and I didn't think I was either. The Bipolar Disorder had been very hard on Kelly and all of us over the last few years. I wasn't ready for this.

The next day, I drove to Kelly's apartment. On the way, I called my niece Angie to tell her what was happening. Angie and Kelly had grown up together and were still close even though she was now living in Dallas. Angie was very concerned. I promised to keep her posted but told her it was probably nothing. I still did not want to believe the possibility of cancer. This was to be the first of many doctor visits that Kelly and I would go to together.

Kelly and I arrived at the surgeon's office, and she began to fill out the forms given to her by the receptionist.

After a minute, Kelly handed the papers to me and asked, "Will you do it for me?"

I took the paperwork from Kelly and quickly filled in the required information. Then I offered her two ibuprofen tablets from the bottle I carried in my purse.

Kelly said, "I'll take them, but it won't do any good."

Kelly moved around in the chair next to me trying to find a comfortable sitting position. The pain in her lower back wasn't making it easy, and I could see her grimace with each move she made.

I handed Kelly the pills and a bottle of water just as the nurse came through the door and called her name. Kelly quickly swallowed the pills and looked at me. When she stood up, I saw the fear in her eyes. I quickly grabbed Kelly's hand and held it in mine as we entered the examining room together.

Kelly walked to the examining table to sit down. I went to the window and stared down at the city. I watched the populace below rushing off to their many destinations and wished Kelly and I could be anywhere else but in that room awaiting our fate. After a couple minutes, Kelly gave up trying to sit comfortably on the table and came to stand next to me at the window.

I smiled at Kelly when she walked toward me and said, "It's going to be okay."

Kelly responded with an uncertain smile, and rested her head on my shoulder.

The doctor entered the room a few minutes later. He was a tall, serious looking man who didn't waste any time. He quickly introduced himself and followed by saying he wanted to schedule a second MRI immediately.

The doctor looked at Kelly and said, "It appears that you were moving around quite a bit during the first MRI. I want to try for a clearer image."

Kelly replied to the doctor by saying, "Yes, it was very hard to lie still with the pain in my back."

He tried to put Kelly at ease by telling her that the enormous lump in her back could be any number of things—and that he would know more at her next visit. Our brief meeting concluded with the doctor leading us to the front desk to schedule the MRI and a follow-up appointment.

Afterwards, I suggested we have lunch. Kelly and I went next door to The Grove – a trendy, outdoor shopping area in the heart of Los Angeles. We were seated right away at one of our favorite Italian restaurants. We ordered lunch, but neither of us ate much.

As we sat there amongst all the beauty and glamour that is L.A., Kelly looked at me and calmly said, "If it is cancer, I'm not going to fight it. I have been asking God to take me for so long, I feel it would be a slap in the face to him if I try to stop it now."

I stared into Kelly's eyes and she stared back into mine. I understood exactly what Kelly was saying to me because she was a part of me. I had witnessed the pain she had endured for the past several years. I had felt every ounce of that pain myself as I tried to take it from her. I wasn't going to sit there now and tell her she had to endure more. That would be selfish. Again, I wished only that I could reach across the table and take it all away, but I knew that I couldn't.

My eyes never left Kelly's while I replied, "So this is gonna be your easy out?"

Kelly softly replied, "Yes," and she slowly turned her face to look away.

We stood up and left the restaurant in silence.

There was nothing easy about what followed over the next three months. Four days later, Kelly was admitted to the hospital for the first time in an effort to relieve the excruciating pain she was dealing with. How strong she had been all that time. The doctors immediately began heavy doses of pain medication but none of it gave her the relief she needed. The biopsy was performed. Kelly was diagnosed with Stage Four Melanoma.

The skin cancer had metastasized and spread from the huge tumor in her back to her hip and groin. Kelly and I sat together on the hospital bed. We stared into each other's eyes once again and I held her hands in mine. I knew that I had to be strong, and I tried to find the right words to say.

Finally I spoke, "They could be wrong, Kelly. We'll get a second opinion."

Kelly replied by silently nodding her head. We soon found out the doctors were not wrong. One doctor after another was assigned to Kelly as they tried to put a plan of action in place. My head was spinning as I tried to process everything the doctors were telling us. I brought the framed photo of Gram that had been on my nightstand to Kelly's hospital room along with Gram's rosary.

I placed them together next to Kelly's bed and said, "We need Gram here with us now."

Kelly's friend Mandy gave me an article about melanoma and tanning beds. The article stated that the use of tanning beds increases your chances of skin cancer by 75%. Mandy and Kelly had been friends since junior high school, and we both knew how obsessed Kelly was with tanning. She'd held a membership card for various tanning salons all through her twenties. She still had one.

I thought back to a time several years earlier when the family was at Lake Tahoe for our annual summer vacation. I remembered the uneasy feeling that had come over me while watching Kelly slather dark tanning oil all over her body and bask in the sun. I told Kelly then that it wasn't good for her, but she shrugged me off. Now I wondered if that had been a premonition.

Then I remembered a phone conversation between Kelly and me about a year earlier, when she had casually mentioned a weird spot on her arm. I told her to have it looked at and she said that she would. It was a few weeks later when I brought it up again and asked Kelly if she had been to the doctor to have it looked at.

Kelly replied, "Oh, no. The spot's gone."

At the time, I thought that was a good thing. Now, as the doctors searched Kelly's body for signs of a starting point for the cancer, I learned that the temporary spot had been the point of entry. It had disappeared once the cancer began to silently creep through her body. Why had I waited three weeks before reminding her to get it checked?

One friend after another showed up at the hospital to see Kelly, and the visits lifted her spirits.

While Kelly and I sat alone in her hospital room one afternoon she said, Mom, I've decided that I want to fight the cancer. I don't want to die."

I was so happy to hear those words come out of her mouth. I hugged her and we prepared for the fight ahead of us. The news we received next was a blow to both of us.

The doctors told Kelly that the cancer had spread too far. There was nothing they could do to stop it. The most they could do for Kelly was to try and alleviate the excruciating pain.

Ron and the boys packed up Kelly's apartment and we moved her back home. A friend gave us the name of a trusted oncologist nearby. She told us that this doctor had saved her life and might be able to do the same for Kelly. We met with the doctor and discussed possibly beginning chemo treatment, but Kelly was getting weaker with each passing day. She would spend the next three months going in and out of the hospital. I was helpless as I stayed by her side wishing I could do more.

Kelly and I were alone at the house one day when she looked at me and said, "Mom, I think I know why Anna was sent to us."

I looked back at Kelly and said, "Tell me."

When Kelly spoke she said, "Since I'm never going to have those kids I always wanted, at least I was able to have Anna as my own for a little while."

I took Kelly's hand in my own and held it. I gave her a tender smile because I knew she was right. Anna had brought so much joy into Kelly's life. At least she had been allowed that. We had always known Anna had been sent to us for a reason.

Chapter Seven

August

Ron and I returned home late in the evening after spending another day at the hospital with Kelly. It had been a rough one for her. The pain was so unbearable that at this point the doctors were keeping her heavily medicated on an intravenous drip. I sat outside in the darkness of the patio trying to process everything that was happening. My precious daughter was lying in a strange hospital bed miles away. Watching my baby girl suffer like that was the worst torment I had ever known. I wanted the doctors to make it stop.

After a few minutes, Ron came out and sat down next to me on the couch.

He put his arm around me and said, "I think we should rent a house down on the beach in Malibu to take Kelly for a few days. It will be good for her."

Ron had been a true father to Kelly, helping her through all of her struggles. I knew Kelly's illness was causing him just as much pain as if Kelly had been his biological daughter. The angels had been listening the day I pleaded for their guidance. He was everything I had longed for in a husband and father to my children. I looked up at him, my eyes full of tears, and nodded my head in agreement. I told Ron I would look online for a rental.

Later that night, I tossed and turned in bed. All I could think of was Kelly, and I gave up on trying to get any sleep. I reached for my laptop that was tucked in between the bed and the nightstand, and tiptoed from the room so as not to wake Ron. I went to the living room and settled onto the couch. My cat, Isaac, followed and curled up next to me. I began the search for rental houses in Malibu. I liked Ron's idea, and thought it would be really good for Kelly to have some time by the water to relax once she came home from the hospital.

I found a little house right on the beach. It was a simple, two-story with a patio that extended out over the sand so far that it gave the illusion of floating over the water. There was a set of wooden stairs that led down to a sandy beach scattered with rocks. The pictures online showed a small tide pool that I thought would give Anna a place to play and search for treasures. I booked the house for the week of August tenth.

We continued going back and forth to the hospital. It was the middle of summer now. The sun was scorching hot, and it was hard to believe this nightmare had only begun in May. Many days, Anna would join us and climb up into the bed with Kelly. It always made them both smile as Kelly pulled Anna close to cuddle with her.

Anna's sixth birthday was approaching in July, and we wanted to try and make the day somewhat cheerful for her. She had been spending so much time at the hospital with us—not an easy task for a little girl. I asked Kelly's friend Mandy if she wouldn't mind spending a few hours with Kelly while we took Anna out, away from the hospital for a little while.

I knew that Mandy wouldn't mind. Mandy had already been there for Kelly almost every single day while she was in the hospital. Mandy would stay there with Kelly all day long, and sometimes just lie in the bed next to her and stroke her hair.

On the rare days when Kelly was feeling a little better, she and Mandy would do goofy stuff to make each other laugh. Once, they even had the cute male therapist who came to take Kelly for a walk laughing at their flirty banter.

Mandy didn't hesitate when I asked about Anna's birthday, so Ron and I took Anna to pick out a new French Bull Dog puppy. She named him Jackson, and he became a huge source of comfort to her during that time—and in the months that followed.

One day, Ron and I spent the day at the hospital while Anna stayed home with Jimmy. Kelly was sleeping a lot due to the medication that was helping to relieve some of her pain. While Kelly slept, Ron and I walked outside to get some air. We sat down at a small, wrought iron table in the shade. Then, Dr. Reid, Kelly's oncologist appeared and asked if he could join us. Ron pulled out a chair and Dr. Reid sat down. He was silent for a moment as he looked at us.

Then he said, "I need to tell you that the cancer is spreading very rapidly. I don't think there's much we can do to stop it. We could attempt chemotherapy, but honestly, it will be very hard on her. I've seen many patients put themselves through the intense treatment required at this stage only to lose the battle in the end."

He said that he thought it best to tell Kelly the truth.

Dr. Reid was a very kind man and you could see in his eyes how hard it was to give us this news. I just stared at him, not wanting to believe he was right—but knowing that he was. I could see what was happening. Kelly's whole right hip was now swollen and bruised. Every day, her body quivered with a damp fever, displaying her immune system's heroic battle against the cancer. But Kelly could barely reach her hand out to Anna anymore. We agreed to meet in Kelly's room the next morning.

We were already there the next day when Dr. Reid arrived. Kelly was awake, but very groggy from the medication. I watched Dr. Reid gently take Kelly's hand in his. Ron and I stood on the other side of the bed and listened to Dr. Reid explain to Kelly with care what he had told us the day before. He told Kelly that he thought she had six months to live, at the most. I held onto Kelly's other hand as she stared back at him.

I watched one single tear appear, and trickle from the corner of Kelly's eye.

Kelly quietly said, "okay."

Kelly slowly closed her eyes, her long lashes so dark against the paleness of her skin. She said nothing else. At that moment I realized how incredibly brave she was.

I left Ron at Kelly's side and followed Doctor Reid out into the hallway.

I touched the doctor's arm to stop him and I asked, "Were you being generous when you said six months?"

He looked into my eyes and said, "Yes."

I thanked him and turned to walk back into the room. Kelly's eyes were still closed, as she squeezed Ron's hand with what little strength she had left in her body. She returned home from the hospital two days later.

Kelly's birthday was approaching. On August third, she would be 34 years old. Since she was home from the hospital again, I thought it might lift her spirits to have some friends over on that day. Kelly liked the idea, and even gave me the names of some of her friends that I wrote down on a sheet of paper. When her birthday arrived, Kelly was so weak that it was a struggle for her to even get out of bed.

I ordered a red velvet cake from a local bakery; it was Kelly's favorite. I asked that they decorate it with red roses and just her name. Kelly loved red roses and even had one tattooed on each of her shoulders. I wanted to make the day special for Kelly, but I couldn't put the usual "Happy Birthday" on her cake. The day was anything but that.

When I picked up the cake, it was as if the pastry chef understood its significance because she brought it out to present it to me herself. The sight of the cake tore deeply at my heart, and a gasp escaped my lips. The entire top of the cake was covered with mounds of gorgeous red roses with dark green leaves. Right in the center of the cake, surrounded by all of the roses, was Kelly's name. It was beautiful, and exactly what I had envisioned—a tribute to Kelly. I wanted my daughter to know how much she was loved. I fought to control my emotions, and thanked the chef for doing such a flawless job.

When I carried the cake into Kelly's room that day, her big brown eyes widened in surprise. The look of pure wonderment on her face for those few short seconds told me I had done it right. She loved the cake and even managed to sit up slightly to take a couple of bites from the piece I cut for her. Kelly's friends were there with her, but for the rest of the day, she slept.

That same week, Kelly's doctor had set up palliative care in our home. The small room that had once been Kelly's teenage haven was now transformed into a hospital room. The antique bed with wooden spindles had been replaced with a metal hospital bed. I placed a comfortable chair right next to the bed for the friends and family that streamed in and out visiting Kelly. The sunlight filtered in through the half-open wooden blinds to reflect off the pale yellow walls. I wished that I could take Kelly back to that time when she was young and carefree. I remembered her sitting on her bed listening to music or talking on the phone. I had tried so hard to help her find happiness and I had failed. Kelly had gone through struggle after struggle only to end up here fighting this battle—and losing. I didn't understand why she had to go through this. It was so unfair, and I was angry. She used to tell me that she thought she was cursed.

I would tell her, "No, Kelly. You're not cursed."

But now, I couldn't help but wonder if she had been right all along.

The picture of Gram and her rosary that I had taken to the hospital now sat on the nightstand next to Kelly. The TV set was tuned to the music channel, playing rock softly in the background. Above the bed hung a small wooden plaque that simply said "Sweet Dreams."

I was sitting in the chair next to Kelly's bed one day when she very calmly pronounced, "I'm going to die in the same room where grandpa died."

It was true. It was the same room my father had passed in seven years earlier. Kelly had made this statement in such a matter of fact way, it was as if she had come to accept her fate. I hadn't arrived at that acceptance yet, and I couldn't even voice a response. I lowered my head in silence.

The next day, I huddled next to Kelly on the bed and her nurse sat in the chair next to us. Kelly was awake, but very weak.

She said, "Mom, I have another one."

My eyes followed Kelly's gaze. She slowly moved the sheet that had been covering her to reveal a huge tumor in the shape of a cigar protruding from the top of her left leg. It must have been 3 inches long and the area around it was beginning to bruise. I knew then that the cancer was continuing to creep silently throughout her body, curling its deadly tendrils into every nook, taking it as its own.

I gently touched the tumor. It felt hard and out of place against the softness of her skin.

I asked, "Is that where it's been hurting so badly?"

Kelly nodded yes, and pulled the sheet back up to cover it. She leaned back against the pillow looking exhausted and defeated. I glanced over at the nurse and our eyes met. She didn't say a word.

The next day the palliative care became hospice care and a new nurse was assigned. The palliative care had not even been in place for a week. That's how fast everything was happening. I knew what hospice care meant because I had been through it with my dad. Still, I pushed that truth deep inside and did what a mother does—I took care of my daughter. And I didn't stop for a minute to think about myself.

Kelly was getting weaker every day, and her brothers were spending a lot of time by her side. Old friends were calling and stopping by all that week as the news spread to each of them. I remember thinking how surreal it was that they were all coming to our home for this reason.

That last weekend, Kelly began to slowly slip away. She was no longer conscious. Her breathing had become shallow and her skin was hot with fever. I kept a bowl of water and a cloth on the nightstand so I could wipe my baby girl's forehead and arms all throughout the day and night. I couldn't give up. I had to try to give her some relief.

Kelly's brother Jimmy sat next to the bed, holding onto her hand, not wanting to let her go. I noticed that her hands were beginning to have a blue tinge to them. She was so pale and thin that her skin appeared to be translucent. I watched Jimmy take out his cell phone and snap a picture of their hands entwined. It was so beautiful, and I could see the depth of the love he felt for his sister at that moment. Then, our eyes met, but neither one of us could say what we both knew was happening. He got up and quietly walked from the room. Kelly and I were alone now and I continued to wipe her brow.

As I wiped, I whispered in her ear, "Please, leave me some dimes."

It was Saturday night when Father Budhi arrived to pray over Kelly. He was a young priest that had just transferred to our parish from the Philippines, and he had a very thick accent. This was Father Budhi's first time administering last rites, and he looked nervous when he walked into the room and took in the scene in front of him. I had tucked Kelly in with a beautiful handmade quilt a friend had made just for her. We were all huddled around Kelly with just the light from a few candles illuminating the small room. I sat in the chair next to the bed with Anna in my arms. She began sobbing uncontrollably the minute the priest started to pray over Kelly. Anna had just had her sixth birthday. She was so young, but so aware of what was happening.

Then, I began to cry. All the tears that I had been keeping locked inside these last three months were now being released and I couldn't stop them. Everything seemed to be moving in slow motion.

I remember thinking, "This can't really be happening."

Monday, August tenth arrived and the house was full of people. Many of Kelly's friends were there and my niece, Angie, had flown in from Dallas to see Kelly one more time. Angie was going to take Kelly's cat, Oliver, home with her. Kelly loved that cat. He was a big, fluffy Maine Coon, all black with big copper eyes, and he would curl up next to Kelly to sleep each night.

Everyone gathered in the dining room at one point looking through old pictures of Kelly that were spread across the table, and I was alone in the room with my daughter.

I held Kelly's hand and I whispered in her ear, "It's okay to let go. Gram is waiting for you."

I just knew that she was. I swear I could feel Gram's presence there, right next to me. I could feel her arms around me, surrounding both Kelly and me with her love. It had to be her giving me strength because I don't know where else it could have been coming from.

Again, I leaned close and whispered to Kelly, "Please leave me some dimes."

Kelly's friend, Ashley, walked into the room at that moment and I stepped out to call the nurse. I wanted to see if there was anything she could do to help Kelly with her breathing. I couldn't bear to see her struggling like that. A minute after I left the room, Ashley frantically called me back. I flew from the kitchen to that bedroom as if on wings.

Kelly didn't make it to the beach house with us.

After three months of hell, going in and out of the hospital trying to get relief from the excruciating pain, Kelly passed from this earth. It was 3:50 P.M. when I watched her take her last breath. I knew the exact time because for some reason, I looked over at the clock on her nightstand. I don't know why I did that, but then I turned to see all the faces of the people crowded around the foot of her bed. They were all staring back at me, their eyes wide and full of disbelief. I looked back at Kelly. She was still.

A wail escaped from my throat, from every pore in my body, and I collapsed over the lifeless vessel that had once held the soul of my daughter. Kelly was no longer there. This was a pain I never knew could exist. I cried like a wounded animal, helpless and alone. I was powerless to stop it.

The crowd silently filed from the room, closing the door behind them. Everyone instinctively knew that I needed to be left alone with my daughter. All my strength was gone. I stayed there with Kelly and wept for a very long time.

The next morning, Ron came to me as I lay in bed not wanting to get up.

He sat down next to me and said, "I think we should go down to the house in Malibu. We have it for the week and I think it will be a good place for the family to gather. The kids can all come down and be with us."

I nodded my head in agreement. But first, Ron and I went together to make the final arrangements.

The service was to be held the following Sunday at a small chapel located on the grounds of the cemetery. I had already found the perfect resting place for Kelly a few days earlier.

When she was alive, Kelly had been afraid of the dark.

One night when I was alone with her, she looked at me and said, "I want to be cremated. And, please don't bury me in the ground. It's too dark there."

I pulled the blanket up closely around Kelly and said, "You're not going to die, Kelly. We don't have to talk about that now."

But I had heard her. When Angie came in from Texas the following week, I took her with me to the cemetery. There, we found a niche high in a curved garden wall at the top of a set of stairs. The wall was made of red brick, with a brownstone ledge that ran across the top. Kelly's niche would be at the very top of a row of eight, several feet away from the ground, just as she had requested.

The next day, we threw a few things in a bag and Ron, Anna and I drove to Malibu. The boys planned to meet us there. I was like a robot just going through the motions. Ron said it was time to go, so I went. Ron told me to get out of the car, so I got out of the car. I was in my own world, completely oblivious to anything going on around me.

Once we arrived at the beach house, Ron told me that the funeral parlor had called to say that Kelly's remains were to be cremated on Thursday morning at 9:00 A.M. They wanted to know if we wished to be present. I stared at him and slowly shook my head no. There was no way I could be there for that. Ron said that he would go. He felt that he should.

The family gathered, and I remember sitting down on that sandy beach while Anna looked through the tide pool, lost in her own sadness.

I stared out at the water crashing on the rocks, asking myself, "Is Kelly really gone?"

A part of me was still hoping it really was just a bad dream.

Thursday morning arrived and Ron left us at the beach to go to the funeral parlor for the cremation. I couldn't think about what was going to take place. I couldn't bear to.

Anna and I had been sitting in the living room with the television on when Ron left. A little while later, I took her upstairs for a bath. I ran the water and put Anna in the tub. Then I realized I needed a towel, so I ran back downstairs. The television was still on, and as I passed by, the screen suddenly went to static. I stopped, walked over and stood there staring at the static on the screen. My eyes went down to the time that was displayed on the cable box right below. It was 9:01 A.M., and I knew that it had happened. I knew, at that very moment, Kelly's energy was being released from the shell that was once her body. It was the exact moment that my daughter's body turned to ash. I watched the static conceal the screen for several seconds before I walked over to turn the television off. We stayed at the beach house for the next four days and the TV never did that again.

The very next day, I received my first dime. I had just washed a load of laundry. The washer and dryer at the rental house were the small, apartment-sized units with the dryer stacked on top of the washer. The dryer was still spinning as I opened the door to take out the clothes, and the dime came flying out at me. I stood there staring down at the dime that I now held in my hand, wondering, *could this really be from Kelly?* I had asked her to leave me dimes, but could it be? Had she really heard me and listened, or was this just a crazy coincidence? I put the dime in my pocket and didn't say a word to anyone.

It wasn't long before more dimes began to appear.

Chapter Eight

Dimes From Heaven

A few weeks after Kelly's passing, Anna and I were home alone staring blankly at the television. I kept expecting Kelly to come walking through the front door dragging her army green duffle bag full of laundry behind her. Suddenly, Anna stood up. I watched her silently walk down the hallway to her bedroom. After a couple of minutes, I got up and followed. As I approached Anna's room, I heard music playing. When I entered the room, I realized the music coming from underneath Anna's bed was Carole King singing *You've Got A Friend*. It was one of Kelly's favorite old songs, and our friend Laura had sung it at Kelly's funeral. Close to two hundred people were there to honor Kelly on that day. Her many friends filled the chapel. Some stood in the back while others watched the service on television screens in the overflow room.

I crouched down to peer under the bed and I saw Anna. She was as far under the bed as possible, with her back pressed against the wall. Anna's IPod was in her hand and she was crying as she listened to the song. I understood exactly how Anna felt because I wanted to do the same thing. I wanted to spend my days hiding in a corner far away from the world outside. But now, Anna was the only reason I got out of bed in the morning.

I coaxed Anna out from underneath the bed and wrapped her in my arms as she cried out, "I miss Kelly."

I held Anna and felt the pain she was feeling. She began to let loose the waterfall of emotions she had been keeping inside her tiny body. We sat there on the bedroom floor together, crying for a long time. She cried for the big sister she had lost. And I cried for my daughter.

When Anna returned to school in September, I spent the days alone in the living room hiding in the big leather chair. I felt safe there. I went back and forth between crying and staring at the wall until one day I ventured out to the grocery store. I walked up and down the aisles, the neatly stacked shelves just a blur. I couldn't focus on anything and my heart began to pound in my chest.

I thought to myself, "What if someone I know sees me? What if they want to tell me how sorry they are about Kelly?"

I couldn't bear the thought of facing anyone. I knew I would burst into tears the minute they mentioned Kelly's name. I bolted from the store and back to the safety of my living room, my hiding place.

Kelly had been a constant by my side since I was sixteen years old and now she was no longer there. We had been more than mother and daughter. We had grown up together. Kelly would call me not just once a day, but several times each day. Now, I sat there alone staring at the phone, willing it to ring.

I needed to hear Kelly's voice on the other end saying, "Hi, it's me."

My phone was silent other than the calls coming in from friends checking on me. But I couldn't answer those calls. Kelly had taken part of me with her when she died. There was now a huge void inside of me that could never be filled. I knew I would carry that emptiness with me for the rest of my life.

I left the house only to drive to the cemetery several times a week or to pick Anna up from school. I stood at that cemetery wall and cried. I wanted to rip the plaque off the wall that was keeping my daughter from me. I wanted to reach inside and take her back. Kelly belonged with me. I told Kelly that I just needed to know she was okay. I had to know that she was safe and that she was happy.

One day, I sat in the leather chair staring out the window at the cars that passed by. I watched my neighbor watering his lawn and wondered how the rest of the world could continue on as if nothing had happened. Didn't they know my Kelly was gone? Then, I noticed a shimmer out of the corner of my eye. I turned my head to look and I saw it on the floor. It was just underneath the opposite window. I stood up and slowly walked across the room to pick up the shiny, new dime that glistened up at me.

I held the dime in my hand and thought, "Why hadn't I noticed it there a minute ago?"

The next day, I found a dime in the covers as I was making my bed. A few days later, I found a dime in the closet next to my shoes. The dimes were beginning to turn up everywhere, but still, I wasn't convinced they were from Kelly.

In November, I made plans to meet two of Kelly's friends for lunch. I wanted to give both of them something special of Kelly's to remember her by. Kelly had lots of cool, fun jewelry that she loved wearing. She had kept the stuff she collected over the years in a tall, standing jewelry box Ron and I gave her for Christmas.

In the week before our scheduled lunch, I went to that jewelry box several times and opened the top compartment to look for a piece of jewelry to give to both of Kelly's friends. Each time, I would slowly open the lid and peer inside. I would touch the different rings or bracelets, and remember Kelly wearing each piece. After a minute, I would snap the lid shut and walk away.

The day before our lunch plans, I decided to try one more time to gather the strength I needed to look through the jewelry. I took a deep breath, sat down on the floor in front of the jewelry box, and slowly started going through the drawers. I pulled out a necklace and caressed it, remembering it around Kelly's neck. I looked at each ring and pictured it on her slender fingers. I went through each drawer working my way up to the top compartment. When I reached the top, I stood up, and slowly opened the lid. As I had done so many times in the past week, I peered inside at all the pieces waiting there for me to choose from. Suddenly, something caught my eye. I saw a dime shimmering up at me from the corner of the compartment. There was no way I could have missed that dime before when I had opened the lid. It had not been there. I knew Kelly was with me at that moment. I felt she approved of the pieces I had chosen to share with her friends. I picked up the dime and squeezed my treasure in my hand.

Before Kelly became ill, Ron and I were tossing around the idea of moving. Now, every time I passed by Kelly's room, I saw the image of her that last day. I found myself turning my face away as I raced past the door.

I knew it was time to move.

Ron agreed and we found a perfect house not far from where we had been living. The house was in need of renovations and the work became a good distraction. I focused my energy on new fixtures, paint colors and flooring over the next three months. Although I was still crying for Kelly every day, I wasn't sitting in the chair staring at the wall. Ron and Anna began to find dimes too, and we received several of them along the way during our renovation.

We were finding so many dimes that I questioned Ron and Anna. "Are you leaving the dimes to make me feel better?"

They were both quick with their replies. "No way!" They both said.

Ron said, "I wouldn't do that to you, Joni."

I believed them. Neither had been in the room with me when I asked Kelly to leave me the dimes. I only shared that moment with them after the dimes began to turn up.

The most miraculous dime came to me on moving day. It is one that I will never forget. Ron and the boys had moved the last load of furniture and boxes out of our old house and I stayed behind to finish cleaning. It had been very hard to go through Kelly's room and pack up her things, but I had done it and I was proud of myself. I placed a sweater and a pair of sunglasses that had belonged to her on the kitchen counter to carry with me. As I prepared to leave the house I picked up both items and placed them on top of my purse.

"I'm taking you with me, Kelly," I said out loud.

I turned to look around the kitchen one last time. As I stood there, I heard something hit the floor in front of me. I looked down to see the dime that lay at my feet. This dime had literally fallen out of nowhere. I reached down to pick it up. I walked over to stand in the doorway of the room where Kelly had passed. I squeezed that dime in my hand and looked around, almost expecting to see Kelly standing there. I didn't see her, but I knew she was there. I felt her presence as if she were standing right next to me. I knew then that what I was experiencing was real. The dimes were real. Kelly was sending them to me just as I had asked her to do that final day her physical body had been alive on this earth. She was listening.

Chapter Nine

Reasons To Believe

Dear Kelly,

It's almost seven months now and I can't get past this. I can't stop crying. I was supposed to leave you my wedding ring—not have you leave me your things. I don't know what to do with it all. Angie is coming in two weeks to help me go through everything. I don't think I can do it.

Are you happy? The only thing I ever wanted for you was happiness. You never found it. I still can't believe you're not here. I miss my phone ringing ten times a day. You're supposed to be calling me. Are the dimes your way of calling? I made an appointment with a spiritual psychic today. I'm hoping to get a message from you. Am I grasping at straws? I need to talk to you.

I can still hear your voice when you were in the hospital getting yet another x-ray. Jimmy and I were standing in *the hallway outside the room waiting for you. When they finished, I heard you say, "Where's my mom?"*

Just remembering that statement makes me cry. "Where's my mom?"

I'm right here, Kelly. Where are you?

*Love,
Mom*

Seven months after Kelly's passing, a brown leather-bound journal caught my eye when I stood in line at the local bookstore. The journal reminded me of one Kelly had used, so I picked it up and placed it in my basket just as I reached the checkout. I soon found myself sitting at my desk each day writing letters to Kelly. Since I no longer had her daily phone calls, this became my way of staying connected to Kelly.

Around that same time, I read an article in the newspaper about a spiritual healer, Olivia, who had written a book on Spirit Guides. She was going to be in my area conducting a seminar followed by a meet and greet. The article was fascinating to me. Olivia told a story of how she had heard a thought loud and clear in her head while standing in line at a movie theater. She described her experience in a way that was almost exactly the same as when I had heard a voice calling my name as a child, and again when I had been guided to go to California. Now, I knew others had experienced the same thing and I wanted to hear more. That familiar nagging feeling returned. I knew this was something I needed to do. I called a friend and we made plans to attend the seminar together.

When we arrived at the venue, I was surprised at how many people were there. We found our seats and listened while Olivia explained ways that each of us could connect with our own guides. It was enlightening to hear various participants share their own experiences with guidance from the other side. When the seminar ended, I noticed a signup sheet by the door for anyone interested in private readings. I wrote down my name and contact information. I received an email from Olivia within a few days to schedule a time for my reading.

I met with Olivia at her home. We greeted each other and I followed her into a small study that held a white whicker table and two chairs set up near a window. We sat down across from each other at the table and my eyes darted around the room, taking it all in. It was a casual, brightly lit room, with sunlight streaming in through the sheer curtains draped loosely at the window. I didn't know what to expect. Kelly and I had watched the psychic medium TV shows together, but I had never done anything like this. I wondered if Kelly was really going to show up. My hands were clasped together in my lap when Olivia began. She told me to take a deep breath and relax. She said I looked very nervous. I agreed that I was. She began to read my "aura" and talk about the colors around me. I didn't pay attention to a word she said. I only wanted to know if Kelly was with me.

As Olivia continued talking, I started to cry.

Finally, I couldn't keep my emotions inside and I cried out, " I just want to know if you see anyone around me."

I told Olivia that I had lost my daughter seven months earlier and I needed to know if she was with me. Olivia was very compassionate and expressed her sympathy. She paused for a moment and said that she was also dealing with someone suffering with Bipolar Disorder. I had not mentioned that Kelly had suffered from Bipolar Disorder, so I was surprised by her comment.

Then, Olivia's whole demeanor changed. She tilted her head slightly as if she were listening to someone speaking to her. She told me that she was being shown Kelly's hands and my hands, and that there was something similar about them.

Olivia looked at me and asked, "Are you wearing your daughter's ring? She's telling me to look at your thumb."

My heart must have stopped beating for a single second because that was my first "Wow" moment. I pulled my hands from under the table and answered yes as I showed her the plain silver band that I was wearing on my left thumb. I wore it there, just as Kelly had worn it for the last ten years of her life. I had put Kelly's ring on the day of her funeral service and had not taken it off since. I wondered how Olivia could have known that.

I was crying so much during this first reading that it was hard for me to process everything that Olivia was telling me.

I do remember asking, "Is Kelly happy?"

Olivia said, "Yes. Kelly is happy and she wants you to know that she's okay."

Olivia told me that Kelly was with me all the time, but she was also looking over two people that were still here on earth—one female friend and one male. Kelly's good friend Mandy came to mind immediately. She had been there every day for Kelly during her illness and I knew that now she was struggling with some personal things in her own life.

I had just run into Mandy by chance the day before. We went to a restaurant and sat together crying and talking about Kelly. I told Mandy about all the dimes Kelly had been leaving for us.

Mandy's eyes opened wide with surprise. She shared with me that she, too, had been finding dimes all over her apartment! I told Mandy that I knew they were from Kelly, which made her happy. I also told her about my scheduled reading with a medium the next day. She was anxious to hear all about it afterwards. When I did make the call to Mandy to tell her that Kelly was watching over her, she was thrilled and comforted to know that Kelly was with her. It also felt good to me knowing that in a way, Kelly was there for Mandy, just as Mandy had been there for her.

Olivia also told me that Kelly was guiding her brother, Jimmy. She felt that he was trying to find his way in life and she was helping him. She wanted him to know that she loved him.

Then Olivia began to speak about Anna.

She said, "Kelly is talking about her little sister, Anna. She loves her very much. She is telling me that Anna is going to be a dancer."

I replied, "Anna takes dance at her school, but she also plays softball."

Olivia continued by saying the dance class Anna was currently taking was too remedial, and she was going to want more of a challenge.

Not long after this reading, Anna did begin to complain that she wasn't learning anything new in dance. She said, "The teacher keeps doing the same things over and over again."

It was obvious that Anna wanted to learn more than what she was being taught, so we moved her to another studio. Dance soon became Anna's one and only passion. She pushed herself and soon become part of the studio's competition team. Every time I watch Anna dance, I can't help but think back to Kelly's guidance that day.

Our reading closed with Kelly saying, "I picked the perfect mom. You loved and supported me through my illness like no one else could have. Thank you, and remember that I love you."

Afterward, I processed the messages I received and I wondered, *"Had Kelly really been there?"*

Chapter Ten

The Dream

Dear Kelly,

Today was Mothers' Day. I hated it—the first one without you here. I went to the cemetery to take you fresh roses from our yard and cried as I stood there. I miss you. You said that you're happy and I hope that's true.

Kelly, thank you for visiting me in my dream last night! You looked beautiful. Thank you for letting me hug you. And thank you for all the dimes.

I love you,
Mom

We were settling into our new home, but I couldn't get the reading with Olivia out of my head. I wasn't sure if my desperation to be with Kelly had convinced me she was there, or if the experience had been real. As if to resolve my confusion, Kelly came to me in a dream. It was like no ordinary dream I'd ever had. I remember Kelly standing several feet away from me, surrounded by the absolute brightest white light I have ever seen. She appeared to be standing with the sun shining directly on her with a brilliance that would blind you in our ordinary world. I could see many figures directly behind Kelly. The figures had no faces or limbs, but were more like bright, white shadows in a crowd right behind her. Kelly and I stared at each other and she smiled. She looked to be around sixteen years old. I remember that she looked absolutely beautiful, in perfect health. Most importantly, she looked happy. Kelly was holding a cup with a straw in her left hand. It reminded me of when she had been here on this earth, always with a fruit smoothie, blended coffee drink, or soda in her hand.

My eyes never left Kelly's. I spoke directly to her, saying, "Kelly, come here so I can hug you."

Kelly looked slightly away from me and to her right for a split second. She appeared to be asking someone for permission. Then, Kelly turned back to face me. She threw the cup in her hand to the ground and came running into my outstretched arms. I couldn't contain my tears as I held Kelly closely. My crying turned to deep sobs. I was holding my daughter in my arms again, and I never wanted to let go. Then Kelly was gone. I was holding onto nothing. There was just darkness as my sobs turned into a wail that awakened me from my sleep.

I sat up in my bed, hoping to see Kelly still standing there. She wasn't there. I saw only the darkness of the room in front of me. I lay quietly back onto my pillow, absorbing what had just happened. I knew that what I had experienced was beyond the realms of my own earthly existence. My daughter had come back to me, or my soul had traveled to the place where her spirit now existed. Either way, I knew that it had not been just a dream. My visit with Kelly had been real, and for that brief moment in time, we had been together again. I was so grateful for the few seconds I had held her in my arms.

When I awoke the next morning, I remembered each detail of our visit. Most importantly, I remembered that Kelly had been smiling. I knew I had been with my daughter again. I would never forget the gift she gave to me that night. The image of her with that big smile will stay with me forever.

The months passed, and dimes continued to turn up everywhere. I would find them in a bin full of towels, or in the middle of the step while I walked upstairs. A dime fell from the kitchen cupboard when I opened the door to put dishes away. I would write in my journal asking for a dime, and have one the next day. Anna would find them when she played in the sand box at school, or under her desk. Ron was finding them, too. We had begun to store them in a cloisonné heart-shaped box that I kept on my dresser. The box was filling up quickly.

One day, Anna sat in my bedroom looking through a wooden memory box of Kelly's things that I kept on my dresser. Ron had given the box to me after Kelly's funeral. It now held pictures of Kelly, her car keys and other everyday items that had belonged to her, which were now mine. I sat with Anna for several moments, picking up different things, touching them and placing them back inside the box. After a few minutes, I left Anna alone with the box and went to dry my hair. When I finished and went back to where Anna had been sitting, she was gone. I called her name and got no reply. I noticed the door to my closet was open, so

I went to the door and looked inside. I saw Anna sitting in a corner of the closet crying. She was wrapped in a sweater that had belonged to Kelly. I sat down next to Anna on the floor, at the same time, pushing an area rug that was stored there out of my way. When I moved the rug, Anna and I both saw the dime that was lying there on the floor in front of us.

Anna looked up at me with tear-filled eyes as I said, "Kelly is here with us."

I picked up the dime and placed it in Anna's tiny hand. She smiled at me, stood up and walked to the dresser to place her dime inside our heart-shaped box.

The next day was July 3. It was Anna's seventh birthday, and Ron and I were going to take her horseback riding as a special treat. The three of us woke up early and drove to a nearby stable. It was a good outing, and I was happy to see Anna smiling as we climbed back into Ron's big Ford truck. We were going to get pizza for lunch. Anna and I buckled ourselves in and Ron started the engine.

Then, Ron shouted excitedly, "Joni, look at the radio display."

My eyes went to the radio where Ron pointed. The radio display that usually showed the name of the song currently being played instead showed the name "KELLY." The three of us were mesmerized by what we saw. The numbers 7: 11 were also displayed right in front of her name. Kelly's name stayed on the display for well over a full minute. We stared at the screen, none of us able to take our eyes away from what we were seeing. Ron quickly pulled out his cell phone and took a picture of the screen. Then, her name disappeared. We had finished our ride at noon, so the numbers in front of Kelly's name could not have been the time of day. I knew that Kelly was there with us at that moment. She wanted to let us know that she was celebrating her little sister's birthday with us. We didn't understand the significance of the numbers 7:11, but soon after that day, Anna began noticing every time the clock was at 7:11.

For months, Anna would call out, "It's 7:11!"

We knew that Kelly was sending her love.

There was no denying the signs we were receiving from Kelly. Although I missed her physical presence, I was beginning to find comfort in knowing that Kelly's spirit was still very much alive.

Chapter Eleven

I Am With You!

Dear Kelly,

 We celebrated your birthday and it was a good day. Everyone was here to honor you. We lit a single candle in your favorite cake. Jimmy took one piece, and with the burning candle in it, placed it in front of your photo. Anna painted a big piece of plywood with a heart and your name on it and Ron hung it in his workshop. I have an appointment with another psychic medium scheduled for a few weeks from now. I feel like you've been orchestrating the whole thing and I can't wait to see if you will show up again. Ron is going with me this time.

 Anna wants me to ask you to leave her another dime. I know we ask for a lot. Thank you for giving me strength.

I love you,
Mom

The day before Anna began second grade, Ron and I took her to school to see her new classroom and find her seat. On the way, I noticed that Anna was quiet in the back seat. I turned to ask what she was thinking about.

Anna said, "I'm thinking about Kelly. Is she going to spend my whole first day of school with me?"

"I'm sure Kelly will be there with you," I said.

After visiting the school, the three of us stopped for breakfast at a restaurant nearby. We followed the hostess to a table and sat down.

The minute we were seated, Anna said, "There's a dime!"

I looked down to where Anna was pointing and saw the dime, right under the table where she was sitting. I smiled as she climbed under the table to retrieve her gift.

"I told you Kelly would be with you tomorrow," I said with a smile.

Anna had gotten the dime she asked for. She also got the comfort of knowing that Kelly would be at her side on the first day of school.

Shortly after Anna went back to school, Ron accompanied me to my second reading with a psychic medium named Allison DuBois. I had read one of her books over the summer, and when I finished the book, I scheduled a private reading with her. I had a strong sense that Kelly had guided me to this reading by the way everything fell neatly into place. I was eager to see if she was going to show up. I still needed proof that Kelly had really been there with me at the first reading. Kelly did not disappoint me. When Allison entered the room and our introductions were made, Kelly quickly made her presence known.

Allison began with, "Your baby girl is here. She's telling me that she loves to have her hair played with."

There was no way that Allison could have known this small detail about Kelly. But it was the statement that followed next that really stunned me.

Allison looked directly at me, and she softly said, "Kelly is talking about your grandmother. She wants me to tell you that she is with her."

I stared at Allison while slowly nodding my head. I had whispered in Kelly's ear that last day that Gram was waiting for her. Now, this complete stranger was telling me that they were together. Allison had no way of knowing that. I was stunned. I knew that I had been right. Gram really had been waiting for Kelly—and she was with her now. I cried and laughed as Kelly spoke through Allison. Kelly told me how she and Gram sat around together eating Fudgesicles and big bowls of candy. In my mind, I saw the very vivid memory of Gram eating one of those Fudgesicles and talking about how delicious it was.

Kelly said that this reading was her gift to me and then she went on to say, "Yes, Mom, I am happy. And no, you are not crazy."

I knew that Kelly's message was a direct reply to all the times I stood at her gravesite talking to her and crying. I would tell her that I just needed to know she was okay, that she had found happiness. I would ask her if I was crazy to think the signs I was receiving were truly from her.

Kelly talked about all of our family during Alison's reading. First, she told Ron that she never wanted him to doubt what he was to her. She told him that she loved him and that he would always be her dad.

Kelly brought up her birthday cake. She said that she liked the cake and to tell Jimmy that she loved him very much. She also brought up the picture that he had taken of their hands entwined.

Kelly spoke of each of her brothers that day, but her most significant message was that her brother, Jeff, was going to have another child—a little girl. Ron and I were both surprised to hear that.

Kelly went on to talk about Anna, her precious little sister.

Kelly said, "Tell Anna that I pinky swear I will never leave her. I was there on her birthday. And the Fourth of July fireworks are for her."

That statement brought a smile to my face because during that time, Anna had been making me pinky-swear to her about something every single day. Also, Kelly had just validated that she had been with us that day in the truck.

Then, Kelly said, "Tell Anna thank you for letting me see life when I was facing death.

Anna was the one thing that kept me going every day and I will always be grateful to her. She brought joy into my life every day."

Allison followed with, "Kelly's talking about your hands. She said there is something similar about her hands and yours."

I held my breath because I couldn't believe this was coming up again.

Then, Allison looked at me and said, "Are you wearing Kelly's ring?"

I immediately held my hand up and said, "Yes!"

It was the second time Kelly had brought up the fact that I was wearing her ring.

Kelly again told me that she was happy and that she was still making people laugh.

Then, Kelly said, "Mom, please start living again." "It's okay to enjoy life without feeling guilty. Please stop just going through the motions while hiding your pain from the rest of the world."

Finally, Kelly brought up the song, *Wind Beneath My Wings by Bette Midler*. I thought back to the day she had played that song for me when she was 15 years old. Now I was crying again. How could Allison have known about that song? How could she have known any of the things she had told us that day?

Christmas was Kelly's favorite holiday. She had always gotten so much enjoyment from lavishing all of us with beautiful gifts. She finished our visit by saying that she wanted us to have a joyous Christmas without sadness.

Kelly said, "I'll be there Mom. I'll be the angel on top of the tree."

Chapter Twelve

Wanting More

Dear Kelly,

I've been doing better since our reading and hearing the things you said. Every day, I go over it in my head in amazement. I was sitting outside on the deck the other evening and I looked up at the sky. The cloud formations were in the shape of a city skyline. It was so beautiful and I wondered if that's where you could be. Where are you Kelly? Did you touch my hand the other morning when I was asleep? I was here alone and I woke up because I felt someone holding my hand. Was it you?

Love,
Mom

Kelly was working very hard to let me know her spirit was with me, but I couldn't get enough. A friend mentioned that a well-known medium by the name of

Rebecca Fearing was going to be giving readings at an event in town. It had only been three weeks since our last reading, but I made an appointment.

The day of the reading arrived. I kissed Anna and I ran out the door, telling her and Ron, "I'll be back after my reading."

This would be my third reading in a six-month period and I couldn't wait to talk to Kelly again. All I could think about was my hope that Kelly would come through this time, too. I walked into the room for the reading, and saw a woman with long, wavy hair sitting at the far end of a small conference table. She watched me come in and close the door behind me.

I took a seat across the table from Rebecca and she said, "I'm a psychic, but I'm also a medium. I speak to people that have passed."

I nodded as Rebecca continued, "You're a mother. You have two children, but you should have three. You lost a child and she is standing right next to you."

I was so surprised by her words that I immediately looked to my right expecting to see Kelly standing there next to me.

I turned to look back at Rebecca. She smiled and said, "She came in with you. She said she likes your sweater."

I looked down and realized that the sweater I had chosen to wear that night had been a favorite of Kelly's. I remembered the many times when Kelly had come to the house and gone directly to my closet to pull out this sweater.

As she put the sweater on, Kelly would always say, "I love this sweater."

I asked Rebecca if she could give me my daughter's name.

Rebecca paused to listen for a moment and replied, "It's Kelly."

At one point, Rebecca said, "I'm confused because Kelly is telling me she was in her thirties when she passed, but that doesn't make sense when I look at you."

I nodded and replied, "I was sixteen when I had her."

Rebecca sarcastically replied, "Yeah, what were you, twelve when you had her?"

A shiver went through my body because I knew that it was Kelly speaking directly to me. We had heard that same line countless times while out shopping together.

Kelly would call out, "Mom," from across the aisle.

Then, it never failed—Someone would look at me and say, "You're her mother?"

I would respond, "Yes."

Then, Kelly and I would exchange glances and wait for that exact line. We always knew it was coming next.

Kelly talked to me so clearly and freely through Rebecca that day, it was as if she were sitting across the table from me. Rebecca even took on Kelly's mannerisms. I saw Kelly in the way Rebecca tilted her head to look at me, in her smile and even in the way she giggled as she spoke. It was the most astounding thing I had ever experienced. I knew that Kelly was channeling through Rebecca and speaking directly to me. Kelly's presence in that room was so strong that I almost felt I could reach out and touch her. Just as she had in two previous readings, Kelly commented that I was wearing her ring.

Kelly talked about when she had been sick. She said that she had been brave through it all, but had really been very scared. I knew that she had been brave, and I was so proud of her.

Kelly said, "My passing wasn't scary, though. It was just like in the movies. There was a long tunnel and at the end of it, Gram and the others were waiting."

Kelly said that they had sat her down in a big chair to calm and welcome her. I asked if she would be waiting there for me when my time came.

Kelly said, "Are you kidding, Mom? I'll be the first one to greet you."

Then, Rebecca said there was a Catholic lady with Kelly from a long time ago. She said the lady was holding a rosary in her hand. I thought of those many nights when I was a child lying in bed with Gram praying the rosary. I knew that Gram was in the room with us. She began to speak to me through Rebecca. Gram told me that she knew how hard it had been for me since losing Kelly, but it was important that I keep my spiritual faith.

Gram said, "My faith is what got me through when I lost my child."

I quietly nodded my head. I knew exactly what Gram was referring to. She had spoken often of the child she miscarried when she was a young woman. The ordeal had been very painful for her.

Rebecca became very excited. She exclaimed, "Kelly said there's a baby girl coming to the family!" She will arrive in the month of June!"

The baby had come up in our last reading, and I couldn't believe Kelly was talking about it again. As far as I knew, there was no one expecting a child in our family.

My reading came to an end. I thanked Kelly and told her that I loved her.

Kelly replied, "I love you, too, Mom. Heaven is a good place. I'm happy. And I'm still laughing!"

The reading was astounding. I stayed up late into the night writing down everything that Kelly and Gram had said. I read and reread every single word. I thought of Gram's message to me and told myself to stay strong.

Knowing that Kelly was with me gave me the strength and courage I needed to take on the task I had been unable to bring myself to do until then. I decided it was time to go through Kelly's things. The many boxes Kelly's brothers had so carefully packed while she was in the hospital had sat untouched in our garage for the past year and a half. With Ron's and my dear friend Sandra's support, I was finally ready to face the task.

The three of us took a deep breath and each began by pulling out one box. I slowly opened the box in front of me, and the first thing to catch my eye was Kelly's journal. I knew that she had kept them on and off for several years. I looked further inside the box and found several more journals. I now held Kelly's deepest thoughts in my own hands. I didn't open the journals right away. I placed them down beside me and continued looking through the box.

Every item I pulled from the box was another memory of Kelly. We spent several hours going through Kelly's things—her life. We went through her books, her music and her clothing - all the "stuff" that she had gathered while on this earth. I found her favorite pair of jeans, with a phone number on a piece of paper still crumpled up in the pocket; sweaters that still held the scent of her favorite perfume. There lay the framed photos of family and friends that had once been scattered throughout Kelly's apartment. There were so many pictures of Anna, or of Kelly with her different friends. In each picture, I saw Kelly's beautiful face staring back at me. It tore at my heart, but I told myself I had to keep going. The process became a little less difficult with each box I opened. After a few hours, I had accomplished something I once thought I would never have the strength to do.

Later, I lay awake late into the night thinking of those journals. I had brought them into my room and placed them behind the chaise lounge in my sitting area. Now, I wondered if I dared read them. Did I have the right to? I wasn't sure. Finally, I got out of bed and walked over to the chaise. I sat down, turned on the light and pulled out the first journal. As I held the journal in my hands, I knew that I needed to see what Kelly had written there. I felt that Kelly was giving me her permission to do so. I slowly opened the cover and stared down at the familiar handwriting on the page in front of me. Then, I began to read.

I read until the early hours of the morning, crying as I turned each page. I read happy entries, but I also found every ounce of pain Kelly had hidden from the world within those pages. I knew that Kelly had suffered, but with each word, I literally felt her pain and the depth of her despair. It ripped my heart wide open all over again. I cried for her.

The next day, I sat in front of the fireplace and burned the pages of Kelly's journals. I would never share those pages with another soul. With each page that I tore from the spine of the journal to toss into the flames, I obliterated another ounce of the pain Kelly had endured while on this earth. As I watched the pages turn to ash, I thought of the readings I had with Kelly. She had told me she is happy now. I kept telling myself that she was.

Over the next few weeks, I felt my resolve slipping away. I didn't want to stay strong or move forward. I spent hours searching the Internet for mediums that would bring Kelly back to me. I hid in my room writing to Kelly in my journal.

"Mommy, will you take me to the park to ride on my bike?" Anna asked through the locked door to my room.

My heart hurt for Anna, but I responded, "Not today, Anna. Ask daddy to take you."

I soon slipped into the deepest depression I had been through yet. I didn't want to leave the shelter of my room. Ron and Anna continued to try and coax me out each day, but I didn't care. I just wanted to know why Gram and Kelly were able to be together—and happy—while I had to be here missing my daughter's presence every day. And why had I not been able to help my child find the happiness she had relentlessly pursued while on this earth? Why hadn't I tried harder? I had failed. I hated myself for that. As I cried, I asked Kelly to forgive me.

The thought of having to wait years until I could be with Kelly again left me wanting to be dead myself. I stood in front of the bathroom mirror, holding the bottle of sleeping pills my doctor had prescribed to me, wondering what it would be like to simply take every one of them.

Just then, there was a knock at the door. "Mommy, will you take Jackson for a walk with me? I want you to come out."

Anna's tiny voice at the door brought me to my senses. I put the pills away.

"Yes, Anna." I replied. "I'll be right out."

That night, I lay awake thinking of Anna. I went to her room and sat on the bed watching her as she slept. She was almost eight years old now. She was so innocent. I looked at her and I realized the amazing gift that I had right in front of me. Anna was here with me now. She needed me to be strong. The love I felt for Anna at that very moment was overwhelming. It was Anna's presence, once again, that gave me the strength I needed to pick myself up and move forward. Gram had known I would need this when she sent Anna to us eight years earlier.

On June 29th of that year, our son Jeff and his wife, Megan, welcomed their new daughter, Delilah Rae Lynn. Delilah was born in June, just as Kelly had promised. Jeff and Megan honored Kelly by choosing her middle name, Lynn, for their daughter. Life continued here.

Anna the Dancer in 2014

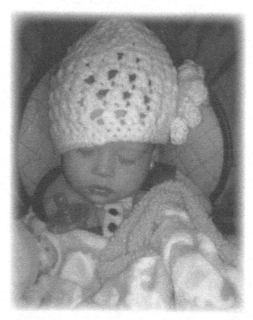

Baby Delilah, born in the month of June, just as Kelly promised.

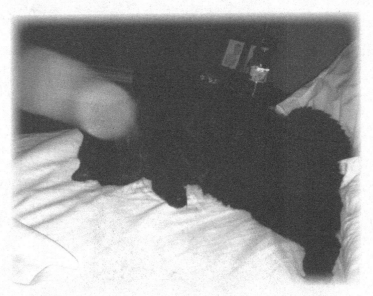

A picture of Kelly's cat Oliver taken in 2011. There is an orb in the picture that appears to be petting him.

Another picture of Kelly's cat Oliver taken the next day. An orb appears in the picture again.

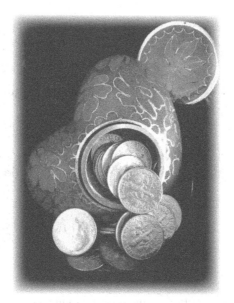

My Box Full of Dimes sent from Kelly

*The picture Jimmy took as he held Kelly's hand,
not wanting to let go of his sister.*

Chapter Thirteen

Let Me Go

Dear Kelly,
I heard you call my name when I was waking up this morning. It was just as I had heard someone call out my name when I was a little girl, only this time, I knew who it was. This time it was you.
You called out, "Mom."
I know you are here. Thank you.
                                                                Love,
                                                                Mom

The New Year arrived. It was 2012, and I found it hard to believe that summer would mark three years that Kelly had been gone. Ron and I had purchased an outdoor couch and placed it on the deck upstairs off our master bedroom. Ron, Anna and I would sit there in the evenings and look up at the stars. It was a peaceful time for all of us. We felt lucky to have found the perfect new home. When I purchased an area rug to place under the couch, Ron and I moved the couch together to place the rug down.

After we moved the couch, Ron looked down and pointed. "Look!" he said, "It's a dime!"

Ron reached down to pick up the dime.

He looked at me and said, "This one's mine!"

Ron stashed the dime in his pocket.

I couldn't help but smile. Ron had started his own dime collection in a box he kept in his office. I was definitely willing to let him have this dime to add to it. He deserved every dime Kelly left for him.

In May, my friend Sandi told me about a gifted psychic/healer she knew. Her name was Ruth Kramer. Sandi had been to see Ruth several times and spoke highly of her. Ruth was going to be in town for a week. I didn't hesitate at the chance to be with Kelly again. Sandi booked an appointment for both of us.

That night, Ron, Anna and I were at the dinner table when I announced my plan to visit another medium. A look of concern came over Ron's face, and he and Anna exchanged glances.

"Joni, are you sure it's a good idea to do this again?" Ron said.

My response was a definitive, "Yes."

There was silence at the table. I knew Ron didn't think it was a good idea. I didn't care. I wasn't going to pass up a chance to talk to Kelly again.

When the evening of the reading arrived, I paced back and forth waiting for Sandi to pick me up. I stood in front of a photo of Kelly and said, "Please, please be there tonight. Get inside her head! I really want to talk to you." As I stood there, I felt Kelly's presence very strongly. There was a sense of urgency in the air.

When we arrived at Ruth's, she looked at me and said, "I need to take you first."

I looked at Sandi and said, "Is that okay with you?"

Sandi agreed immediately. "Of course!" she replied.

I sensed the same feeling of urgency that had surrounded me at home when I followed Ruth into her office to begin our reading.

Kelly began speaking through Ruth the minute we entered the room.

"She has a lot she wants to say to you." Ruth commented as she sat down across from me.

Kelly said, "I couldn't stay here on this earth. Everything was too hard for me here, such a struggle. It wasn't your fault, Mom. That's just the way it was for me."

I understood what Kelly was saying and I quietly nodded my head. Kelly continued to speak. What she said next astonished Ruth and me.

Kelly said, "Where I'm at now is amazing and beautiful, Mom. From where I am, I can see all the planets in the universe beautifully lined up. I am flying free with wings like the birds and butterflies. I am able to do everything that I couldn't do there. I'm learning so many new and wonderful things about the universe and I want you to know how happy I am."

Ruth commented, "I never knew where the spirits were before!"

Ruth became even more excited by what Kelly told us next.

Ruth said, "There's going to be a wedding! Oh, it's there–it's her! She's getting married!"

I was stunned by what Kelly was revealing to us. Had I heard Ruth correctly? My daughter was getting married? But Ruth continued, telling me Kelly's fiancé's name was Robert. He was someone Kelly had known from school. Ruth said that his passing had been after Kelly's.

Kelly explained, "It's not going to be like a wedding there, but more about our spirits coming together. Robert is my soul mate and we will be together forever."

Then, Kelly told me to pay close attention to my dreams because she was going to try and take me there for the wedding. Kelly's words were overwhelming, and I cried as she continued.

Kelly brought up my journals to her and said, "Your journals would make a great book, Mom. If you share them, other people will know that they never really lose their loved ones." Kelly continued by telling me that I needed to start breathing again. She said that I hadn't really breathed since she left, and she wanted me to start.

Kelly said, "I want you to go on and live your life and be happy, Mom. You still have a lot of work to do there, but when the time is right, we will be together."

Once again, Kelly brought up her ring. She knew I wore it as she did. I know that mentioning the ring each time was Kelly's way of saying, "Yes Mom, It's really me."

Then, Kelly asked something of me.

Kelly said, "Mom, I need your acceptance. I ask that you let me go."

She continued by saying, "I know that you think about me all the time. I think of you, too. But, I'm so busy with all these amazing things happening that I need for you to set me free."

I knew why Kelly was asking this. For almost three years, she had been there for me, trying to console me in my anguish. She had answered my constant begging for signs that she was with me over and over again. I knew in my heart that I had to do what she asked of me—I had to let her go.

When the reading ended, Ruth and I looked at each other, both of us stunned by what we had learned.

Ruth commented, "I feel like Whoopi Goldberg in the movie *Ghost*! I have never had a spirit come through me so strongly with so many things to say!"

The experience had been beautiful. I was still crying when our reading came to an end. Ruth and I walked out of the room together and I began to relay everything Kelly had said to Sandi. Ruth smiled and handed me a pen and paper to write it all down.

I understood completely what Kelly was asking of me. I had to accept that she was gone from this earth, but know that her spirit would always be with me. She needed for me to let her go in order to move on, learn and grow. I knew that I had to do what she asked. I had to stop crying, begging for signs and needing validation from her every second of every day. Gram had told me to keep my spiritual faith and believe that we would be together again some day. I had to do it for Kelly. And I know she also wanted me to do it for myself. I just wasn't sure if I could.

Later that same night, Kelly was still with me. I was awakened from my sleep at two a.m., when Anna climbed into bed with Ron and me, as she often does. While waking up, I felt myself being pulled away from Kelly. I can't remember what we had been doing, but felt very strongly that I was being pulled away from her. Anna got under the covers and fell asleep immediately. I was wide-awake, and I could feel Kelly all around me. Her presence was so strong that I actually sat up twice and stared into the darkness of the room expecting to see her standing there. I didn't see her, but her energy was so powerful that I had a high-pitched ringing in my ears. I lay back down and Kelly stayed there with me for a very long time. I lay there, trying very hard to take myself back to wherever that place with Kelly had been, but I couldn't. Eventually, I fell back to sleep with Kelly's energy all around me. I never got back to that place, at least that I can remember. I still wonder if Kelly had been trying to take me to her wedding. I know it sounds crazy, but she had promised to during our reading. I honestly believe Kelly had tried to share that special moment with me.

Chapter Fourteen

One More Reading

Dear Kelly,
I know you're sending me signs that you're okay, but I still miss you. I'm trying. Today, the sadness was overwhelming. I went to the cemetery and sat there for a long time. I don't know what to do. Please leave me a dime.

Love,
Mom

The months passed. I thought I had come a long way with acceptance, as Kelly had asked me to do—until I went back and started reading my journal. I was crying less often, trying very hard to let her go. I was trying to find acceptance and comfort in the knowledge that Kelly was truly happy. But, I was still asking her for signs constantly within the pages of my journal.

Sandi and I were having lunch together when she told me about another medium named Roe Tomlin who would be in town. I thought about Kelly asking me to give her space to move on, so I tried to tell myself not to make an appointment with Roe. I had promised Kelly I would try to let her go, but it was so hard to be away from her.

After all, I told myself, *eight months have passed since my last reading. One more reading couldn't hurt.*

Kelly was my daughter. I wanted her with me. I booked an appointment with Roe.

Sandi also made an appointment. The night of the readings, we drove together. We walked into the office and saw Roe seated behind a high counter. Roe stood, greeted us both and we made our introductions.

Then, Roe smiled warmly and said, "There's a young woman with you."

Sandi and I exchanged knowing glances. We both knew whom Roe was referring to. Kelly was already there with us. Sandi knew Kelly well. It was Sandi's daughter, Mandy, that had been there for Kelly at the hospital every day. When the girls were younger, Kelly had spent a great deal of time at their house and Sandi had been very good to her.

Sandi and Roe went into a small office to begin her reading. I waited in the outer area. We had both scheduled one-hour appointments, so it was hard for me to sit patiently for that amount of time. I couldn't wait to talk with Kelly. At one point, I stood up and began pacing back and forth in the waiting area. I passed the door to the office Sandi had gone into, and heard Roe say that the spirit of a young woman was telling her she had passed from cancer three years ago. I knew that Kelly was spending time visiting with Sandi. Although I was happy for Sandi, I couldn't wait to get in that room. I sat back down. Soon, I felt Kelly's presence next to me in the waiting area.

When it was my turn, I hugged Sandi as we passed each other. I entered the office and sat down at a small table. Roe was seated directly across from me. She began by saying she knew it was my daughter in the room with us, and that Kelly was eager to talk with me.

Kelly was in a very good mood as the reading began. Roe kept laughing and talking about how nutty Kelly was being.

Roe said, "I just love her personality!"

This was the Kelly we all loved and missed so much. It was good to hear that she was happy. I was afraid she might be upset with me for booking another reading.

When Kelly started talking to me she said, "Hi Mommy. I'm glad you're here!"

Roe commented, "How sweet it is that Kelly's calling you mommy."

Once again, Kelly had a lot she wanted to say to me. The mood in the room was very lighthearted as she continued to speak through Roe.

Kelly said, "I know that you don't think you were a good mother, but you're wrong. I'm proud of you Mommy, and I would choose you again. I love you so much and I am always, always with you. I didn't leave you on purpose. I want you to stop grieving and be happy."

The room was filled with the intensity of Kelly's presence. I could feel the love she was sending without question.

Just then, Roe asked, "Did you feel that? Kelly just hugged you."

I nodded my head, yes.

Kelly said that she had tried to visit Anna in a dream. She wanted me to tell Anna that she tucks her in every night after I do, and kisses her good night.

Kelly said, "Be sure to tell Anna that I love her!"

Gram was also with us that night. Roe said she was referring to me as "My Joni."

Gram said, "Tell my Joni that I love her."

That was how Gram had always referred to me when she was here on earth.

I beamed while I replied, "I love you, too, Gram."

When Kelly began to speak to me again, she brought up my own mother—the mother that had left me when I was eight years old. My niece, Angie, had let me know of her passing about a year after Kelly's passing. At the time, the only emotion I felt was anger. I didn't want her near my daughter.

Kelly said, "I've seen your own mother here."

My reply was simple and to the point. I said, "I don't want to talk about her."

Kelly was quick to respond with, "You know, Mom, if she hadn't left, you wouldn't have had Gram."

Although Kelly's words held truth in them, I had nothing to say. I remained silent.

Kelly continued to chide me. For three years, I had been going to the cemetery two or three times every week. At this point, I was still going once a week to sit at Kelly's gravesite.

Kelly's exact words were, "Stop going to the cemetery, Mom. I'm not there."

"Kelly is insisting that you write a book with your journals," Roe said. "She wants you to share them with others, so they will know they never really lose their loved ones."

Kelly had mentioned this to me at my last reading, but I didn't pay much attention to it. Then Roe repeated the statement again, saying, "Kelly is insisting that you write this book for her. She also wants you to continue to get the word out about the dangers of tanning beds."

Kelly said, "Use my Facebook page for something other than saying, 'Happy Birthday' to me. By doing these things, you will be giving meaning to the life I had on earth."

Then, Kelly scolded me. She said, "Mom, if you don't start listening to me, I'm going to stop showing up."

Kelly's words stung at first, and I thought, *how could she say something so hurtful to me?*

Kelly continued to reprimand me, saying "Stop spending your money on this if you aren't going to listen to what I'm telling you."

The sting that had come from the honesty of Kelly's words only lasted for a few seconds.

Kelly quickly added, "I love you, Mommy. Whenever you hear the song *Wind Beneath My Wings*, think of me and know that I'm playing it for you. That's still my song to you."

As Kelly began to step back, Roe described what she was seeing in front of her. Kelly was walking away, but before she did, she turned to look back.

Kelly looked over her shoulder and said, "Mom, good night! Sleep tight! Don't let the bed bugs bite!" as she giggled and walked away.

Chapter Fifteen

Fly Away

Late that night, I couldn't sleep. I went over everything Kelly had said to me. She had told me so much and there was absolutely no doubt in my mind that every word had come directly from her. I knew that this time, I had to listen to Kelly. She had been listening to me. She had given me everything that I asked of her. Now, it was my turn. I had to take Kelly's gifts and live my life to the fullest while I remained on this earth. I had to keep the faith. I pulled out my journal and wrote to Kelly one more time. This time, I wrote:

> Dear Kelly,
> I know I wasn't a perfect mother. I was young and I made mistakes. I want to thank you for your forgiveness. I'm sorry I didn't let you go when you asked me to. I know you understand it was the mother in me that couldn't set you

> free. In a way, you and I switched roles. For three years, you have been by my side, working relentlessly to take away my pain. You were so patient with me as you guided me through my grief. Thank you.
> Now, it's my turn. I'm setting you free. Fly, Kelly!
>
> Love,
> Mom

The next day, I began typing the pages of my journals—and I stopped crying. Kelly set me off me on the journey of writing this book, knowing that it would heal me. As I typed, it became very clear to me how much I demanded of Kelly. And that she never once let me down.

In the days and months that followed, I stopped going to the cemetery weekly. I even began to really laugh again. Ron and I planned a fun trip with Anna and our grandkids to an amusement park in Hollywood. We stayed overnight at a hotel near the park and turned it into a two-day outing. The kids had a blast on the rides and we explored the park together.

When we sat together at dinner that night, Ron looked at me and said, "It's good to see you smiling again."

I agreed with Ron. It felt good to laugh.

A few months later, my friend, Sandra asked if I would like to help put together a team to walk in the American Cancer Society's Relay for Life event that was coming up in our town. Sandra had asked me to do this a year earlier. At that time, there was no way I could have gotten through something like that. I told her I couldn't do it. This time, I decided to give it a try.

We put together a great team of friends and family. Anna came up with a name for our team.

She was so excited when she said, "Mommy, I know what we can call our team! We can call it *Soul Sisters* in honor of Kelly."

"That's perfect!" I said.

Anna worked hard getting sponsors. I made up brochures with a photo of Kelly on the front warning girls of the dangers of tanning. The brochure was full of statistics that I had pulled from various websites. I handed the brochures out to participants that visited our booth at the event. I was even able to tell a few young girls and their mothers that it was my daughter on the front of the brochure. I felt that I made an impact. One young lady told me that she was happy someone was getting the word out about the dangers of tanning. Knowing that I may have stopped a few young girls from using tanning beds felt good, and I knew that Kelly was proud of me. I was listening.

It took me quite a while, but with Kelly's help, I survived what I thought I couldn't. I am so grateful to Kelly for that. I know that she wants me to live my life and be happy. I now realize that I owe it to her to do that.

But mostly, I owe it to her to let her go.

I still think of Kelly every hour of every day. And some days I do cry. I visit the cemetery occasionally to place flowers there for Kelly because it's something I like to do for her. When I feel the tears welling up inside, I think of Gram telling me to "keep my spiritual faith." That statement gets me through. There is no doubt in my mind that Kelly's spirit carries on. And I know that Gram is still taking care of her for me.

I know these things because Kelly has proven to me over and over again that life does go on in this amazing universe in which we live.

Kelly asked me to share these journals so that other people would know that we never really lose our loved ones. If we listen closely, we will hear them. If we see a sign we think is from a loved one, believe it. The signs are real. They are there to help us through.

I think of how Kelly ended our last reading by repeating what I used to say to her every night when she was a little girl:

"Good night! Sleep tight! Don't let the bed bugs bite!" as she giggled and turned to leave.

This is my Kelly. I know that she's watching over me and I know that she is happy. When the time is right, I will see her again. I'll be able to take her in my arms and hold onto her forever. I tell myself to be patient. For now, I know that I'm letting her fly free like the birds and the butterflies.

Epilogue

Ron and I sit on the deck one night, looking up at the stars. Anna comes to join us as she hands me a dime.

"Look what I found," she says with a smile.

Then, Anna looks up at the sky and says, "Did you know that when the stars come out at night, it's the angels opening their windows? They're looking down from Heaven and watching over us."

Then, I smile.

This is the one page of Kelly's journal that I saved. I know that this is exactly how she must be feeling at this very moment, and I never want to forget that. I have also included a poem she wrote to me on Mothers' Day, 2004:

Hawaii 2004
Today I had a revelation – seriously...went running this morning with Jim, Jeff and Trina and ended up on these really high cliffs overlooking the ocean. We stood on top of the cliffs and felt the breeze blowing on us and the waves would crash and come all the way up and spray us. It was the most beautiful thing I'd ever seen. The water was bright blue and green, so unbelievably gorgeous. I stood there feeling so free and healthy and clean and SANE and I realized - this is what people mean when they say, "life is beautiful". I never want to forget that feeling.

What a sacrifice you made all those years ago
To take a chance on a baby girl that you didn't yet know

Your spirit already fragile from abandonment of your own
Your heart still willing to give, although you were alone

The courage it must have taken to rise above the strife
Giving all that you had to give to this tiny new life

You chose to be a mother, the hardest task of all
And despite your many obstacles, came out standing tall

I wonder if you know the depth of this little girl's pride
Or how much you inspire me when I feel hopeless inside

And do you know how sweet it is to feel admiration so deep?
I'm lucky enough to know, because it's me you chose to keep

I love you, mommy - Happy Mothers Day!

Kelly
2004

A very special Mothers' Day Gift I received from Kelly

The U.S. Department of Health and Human Services and the World Health Organization's International Agency for Research on Cancer have classified UV radiation from tanning devices as carcinogenic (cancer-causing) to humans, in the same category as tobacco and tobacco smoking. Another fact states, "Those who had been exposed to UV radiation from indoor tanning before the age of 35 increased the risk of Melanoma by 75%

SAMHSA's National Helpline
SAMHSA's National Helpline (also known as the Treatment Referral Routing Service) is a confidential, free, 24-hour-a-day, 365-day-a-year, information service, in English and Spanish, for individuals and family members facing mental health and/or substance use disorders. This service provides referrals to local treatment facilities, support groups, and community-based organizations. Callers can also order free publications and other information.
Call 1-800-662-HELP (4357) or visit the online treatment locators.
The service is open 24/7, 365 days a year.

If you are thinking about harming yourself or attempting suicide, tell someone who can help right away:
- Call your doctor's office.
- Call 911 for emergency services.
- Go to the nearest hospital emergency room.
- Call the toll-free, 24-hour hotline of the National Suicide Prevention Lifeline at **1-800-273-TALK (1-800-273-8255)** to be connected to a trained counselor at a suicide crisis center nearest you.

The National Institute of Mental Health (NIMH) is part of the National Institutes of Health (NIH), a component of the U.S. Department of Health and Human Services.

CPSIA information can be obtained
at www.ICGtesting.com
Printed in the USA
LVHW091952250223
740344LV00018B/75/J